Islam and Women

A New Approach

Āyatullāh Sayyid
Munīr al-Khabbāz

AL-BURĀQ

Copyright

ISBN: 978-1-956276-19-0
Printed and published by al-Burāq Publications.

These chapters are abridged lectures given by Āyatullāh Sayyid Munīr al-Khabbāz in the nights of Muḥarram, 1443 A.H [August 2021]. His Eminence reviewed and approved the content of these adaptions as transcribed and adapted by Brother Ḥasan Hānī Āl-Sayf.

Where needed, context and transliterations were added. Some minor edits were made to the translated Arabic text.

Ordering Information
We offer discounts and promotions for wholesale purchases, non-profit organizations, and other educational institutions. Contact us at the email below for further information.

www.al-Buraq.org
publications@al-Buraq.org
First Edition | June 2022

Dedication

The publication of this book was made possible through the generous support of our donors.

Please recite *Sūrat al-Fātiha* and ask Allāh for the Divine reward (*thawāb*) to be conferred upon the donors and also the souls of all the deceased in whose memory their loved ones have contributed graciously towards the publication of *Islam and Women: A New Approach.*

We begin by giving all praise and thanks to God ﷻ for giving us the tawfiq to translate this book. He has guided us and without Him, we would not have been guided to the straight path embodied by the Prophet Muḥammad ﷺ and the Ahl al-Bayt عليهم السلام.

This book is firstly dedicated to Āyatullāh Sayyid Munīr al-Khabbāz, and is also dedicated to all the scholars, martyrs and believers who worked tirelessly to promote the pure Muḥammadan path.

We want to also give our thanks and appreciation to all believers from around the world and acknowledge the team which helped al-Burāq Publications complete this work, spending countless hours to make its publication possible. Please recite Sūrat al-Fātiḥah on behalf of them and their marḥūmīn.

This book is dedicated in honor of the following individuals. Please remember them in your prayers and may God ﷻ have mercy on them and their loved ones.

Ali Al Barak

Ali Ftouni

Aliya Haider

Alya Agemy

Amine Yazback

Badrul Hasan Jafri

Bande Khuda

Basheerunnisa Begum

Hadi Ali Hijazi

Haj Abed Hammoud

Haj Ahmad Daoud

Haj Haidar Alaouie

Haji Hoda Sharara

Haji Nawal Najdy

Haji Sobhia D. Aoun

Hajj Ali Hammoud

Hajj Hassan Sobh

Hajj Sami Ftouni

Hajji Amneh Sobh-Ftouni

Hajji Hiam Hojeije

Hajji Iman Elsaghir

Hajji Imane Srour

Hassan Baker

Humayun Baig

Ibrahim Habib

Ibtisam Hammoud

Mahmoud Farhat

Meerna A. Aoun

Mohamad Shebley

Mohsin Jafri

Munawwar Jehan

Noor Sakha

Nour Hijazi

Radhiya Alqallaf

Sabiha Jafri

Sanjuana Rocha

Sayyid Sobh H. Sobh

Shandaar Fatima

Syed Ali Zaidi

Syed Mehdi Rizvi

Syed Nawab Kazmi

Syed Nurul Jafri

Turfah Sobh

Duʿāʾ al-Ḥujjah

اللهم كن لوليك الحجة بن الحسن صلواتك

عليه وعلى آبائه في هذه الساعة وفي كل

ساعة وليا وحافظا وقائدا وناصرا ودليلا

وعينا حتى تسكنه أرضك طوعا وتمتعه فيها طويلا

O God, be, for Your representative, the Ḥujjat (proof), son of al-Ḥasan, Your blessings be upon him and his forefathers, in this hour and in every hour: a guardian, a protector, a leader, a helper, a proof, and an eye - until You make him live on the Earth, in obedience (to You), and cause him to live in it for a long time.

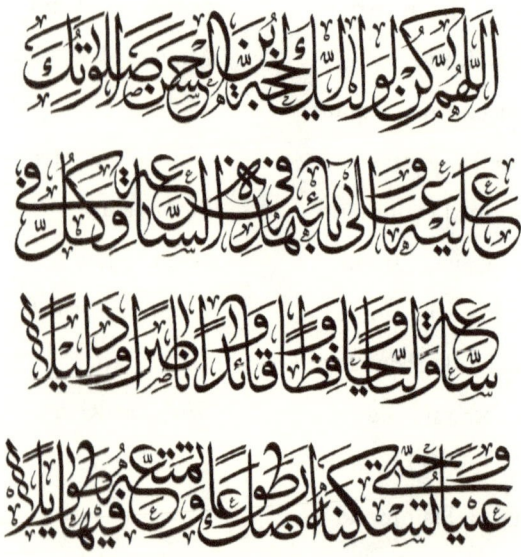

Terms of Respect

The following Arabic phrases have been used throughout this book in their respective places to show the reverence which the noble personalities deserve.

عزّ وجلّ

Used for God, meaning:
Exalted and Sublime (Perfect) is He

صلى الله عليه وآله

Used for Prophet Muḥammad, meaning:
Blessings from God be upon him and his family

عليه السلام

Used for a man (singular) of a high status, meaning:
Peace be upon him

عليها السلام

Used for a woman (singular) of a high status, meaning:
Peace be upon her

عليهما السلام

Used for men/women (dual) of a high status, meaning:
Peace be upon them both

عليهم السلام

Used for men and/or women (plural) of a high status, meaning:
Peace be upon them all

قدس سره

Used for a deceased scholar, meaning:
May his resting [burial] place remain pure

عجل الله تعالى فرجه الشريف

Used for Imām Muḥammad al-Mahdī, meaning:
May God hasten his return

Transliteration Table

The method of transliteration of Islamic terminology from the Arabic language has been carried out according to the standard transliteration table below.

ء	ʾ	ر	r	ف	f
ا	a	ز	z	ق	q
ب	b	س	s	ك	k
ت	t	ش	sh	ل	l
ث	th	ص	ṣ	م	m
ج	j	ض	ḍ	ن	n
ح	ḥ	ط	ṭ	و	w
خ	kh	ظ	ẓ	ه	h
د	d	ع	ʿ	ي	y
ذ	dh	غ	gh		
Long Vowels					
ا	ā	و	ū	ي	ī
Short Villages					
ـَ	a	ـُ	u	ـِ	i

Table of Contents

About the Author

Āyatullāh Sayyid Munīr al-Khabbāz was born in Qatif, Saudi Arabia in 1384 AH (1964 CE). At the age of 14, Sayyid Munīr traveled to the Holy City of Najaf to begin his training within the Islamic seminary. Not long after, he migrated towards the city of Qum, Iran, when the Baathist Regime in Iraq began tightening its crackdown on the Islamic seminary.

In the year 1402 AH (1981 CE), Sayyid Munīr returned to Qatif for personal reasons and continued his studies there. One year later, he traveled to Damascus, Syria to study in the Islamic seminary there under the tutelage of His Eminence Sayyid Jamāl Khū'ī. Finally, in 1405 AH (1984 CE), he returned to the Holy City of Najaf to continue his studies. There, he studied under some of the most respected scholars of the Islamic seminary, including Āyatullāh Sayyid Abū al-Qāsim Mūsawī Khū'ī and Āyatullāh Murtaḍā Burūjirdī. With the recommendation of another one of his tutors, Sayyid Ḥabib Ḥusaynian, Sayyid Munīr also began to study under the tutelage of Āyatullāh Sayyid 'Alī Sistānī, benefitting much from his lessons in the principles of jurisprudence, as well as his extensive examination of modern sciences and their correlation with Islamic sciences.

Sayyid Munīr then moved back to Qum where he studied under Āyatullāh Waḥīd Khurāsānī for several years. He also studied extensively under the tutelage of Āyatullāh Mīrzā Jawād Tabrīzī, who became a guide and mentor for the remainder of his life. Before his passing,

Āyatullāh Tabrīzī gave Sayyid Munīr an endorsement as a jurist capable of deducing Islamic laws from its sources.

In 1418 AH (1997 CE), Sayyid Munīr began teaching Advanced Seminars (Bahth Kharij) in jurisprudence. He is known by his students for his eloquence, as well as his encouragement of discussion and debate. He is an avid lecturer and an author, with multiple works published for a varied readership.

Foreword

بسم الله الرحمن الرحيم

In the Name of God, the Beneficent, the Merciful

In this book, Āyatullāh Sayyid Munīr al-Khabbāz delivers twelve lectures on a wide variety of topics. Although the lectures were delivered during ʿĀshūrāʾ, Sayyid Munīr does not limit himself to historical events. Rather, he uses the topic of ʿĀshūrāʾ to approach various topics that are of interest to the contemporary Muslim. His new approach proves that ʿĀshūrāʾ really is for every time and place, and that it has insights to offer in a variety of fields. Instead of dealing with ʿĀshūrāʾ as a past historical event, Sayyid Munīr's depicts it as an ever-present phenomenon within Islam.

This present book deals with topics as diverse as the methodology of discussing Islam, the hijab, women's rights, the status of women in Islam, gender identity, family life, raising children, the duty of parents, the ideal married life, and being a leader and a successful figure. Sayyid Munīr utilizes a unique approach to get his message across, using Sayyidah al-Zahrāʾ and Sayyidah Zaynab عليهما السلام as pivots for his discussion. Above all, Sayyidah al-Zahrāʾ عليها السلام is the common thread, whether as the perfect human being in and of herself, the daughter of Islam's Prophet ﷺ, the mother of the pure and brave Sayyidah Zaynab عليها السلام, the mother of the other Imāms عليهم السلام, or the wife of ʿĀlī عليه السلام. In turns,

Sayyidah al-Zahrāʾ ﷺ emerges as eloquent, courageous, virtuous, pious, and, despite her sorrows, ultimately triumphant. This book is a reminder of the relevance and importance of Sayyidah al-Zahrāʾ ﷺ not only in history, but for our times as well. Through her, we strive to become better Muslims, as she is a role model for male and female Muslims alike. She reminds us to value the courage and sacrifices of the women in our lives, and her life is a living example of how women should live and how men can support and uphold the women in their lives, including but not limited to daughters, mothers, and wives.

Biography of Sayyidah al-Zahrā’ عليها السلام Between Verification and Sectarian Manipulation

How can we approach history? There are three methods of approaching history: the descriptive approach, the analytical approach, the verification approach.

The descriptive approach is transmitting the incidents of history like they have been narrated as long as they don’t contradict reason, such as narrating the incidents of the death of Imām al-Ḥusayn عليه السلام in Karbalā’ as they have been transmitted.

The analytical approach is analyzing history: its causes, consequences, periods, and influential incidents. This approach includes three methods: the humanistic method, the anthropological method, and the faith-based method. All of these methods can be applied to the biography of Sayyidah al-Zahrā’ عليها السلام for example.

The Humanistic Method

This method is preferred by the pioneers of modernism. It considers the human being as a human being without any other additions. However, some scholars like Muḥammad Arkūn, Salāma Mūsā, and ‘Alī Ḥarb separate the human being from religion and the sacred. They say that one cannot read man as a religious being or as a believer in a religion, as that constitutes a misunderstanding of modernism. This is because a religious person lives in submission to God ﷻ whereas modernism gives primacy to the human without any other associations. However, this is an extreme view because modernism itself does not clash with reading man as a religious entity. Sometimes, it reads the human with respect to his religious motives only, and at other times it reads the religious human being through the humanistic motives that cause him to approach religion. This is a humanistic understanding. If we want to understand the biography of Sayyidah al-Zahrāʾ ﷺ, we can do it through the humanistic method: "They fulfill their vows and fear a day whose ill will be widespread. They give food, for the love of Him, to the needy, the orphan and the prisoner."[1] Sayyidah al-Zahrāʾ ﷺ gave charity because she felt the worries of humanity and society. When we consider Sayyidah al-Zahrāʾ ﷺ as a housewife, we also do so from a humanistic view. When her father the Prophet of God ﷺ entered and saw her turning the millstone with one hand and holding her infant son with the other, he ﷺ cried at the sight. She ﷺ replied, "Praise be to God for His blessings, and thanks be to God for His bounties," expressing a spirit that's full of patience, confidence, and contententment (*qanāʿa*). This is a humanistic reading; humanism is to read a human being in their hopes and pains; the pains of their society and the hopes of its salvation. This was Sayyidah al-Zahrāʾ ﷺ; how can she not be like this when she was the daughter of the man about whom God ﷻ said, "There has certainly come to you an prophet from

[1] Sūrat al-Insān, verses 7-8.

among yourselves. Grievous to him is your distress; he has deep concern for you, and is most kind and merciful to the faithful.”[2]

The Anthropological Method

The philosopher Kant defines this method as “a doctrine of knowledge of the human being.”[3] Anthropology means reading society in a multi-dimensional way by considering the economic, cultural, and religious aspects of a given society. This multi-dimensional reading is an anthropological reading. Can we read Sayyidah al-Zahrā’ ﷺ through this method? The states that colonized the Third World, such as France and Britain, have read societies in an anthropological way, considering their habits, traditions, religions, sects, and cultures for the purpose of colonizing them. Every multi-dimensional reading of a society is a directional reading; we can read Sayyidah al-Zahrā’ ﷺ from this angle. When we consider the sermon of Sayyidah al-Zahrā’ ﷺ, she went to the mosque, placed a cover between her and the people, and gave that well-known eloquent sermon of hers. This

[2] Sūrat Yūnus, verse 128.

[3] Translator’s note: See Immanuel Kant, *Anthropology from a Pragmatic Point of View*, translated and edited by Robert B. Louden with an introduction by Manfred Kuehn (New York: Cambridge University Press, 2006), 3.

sermon expresses three important factors in Sayyidah al-Zahrā''s 🌸 character:

1. The first is the cultural factor. It is a sermon brimming with culture and a deep understanding of Islam in its principles, branches, dimensions, and achievements. This means that the sermon expresses a cultural dimension in Sayyidah al-Zahrā's 🌸 character.

2. The second factor is mobility. She was a woman who went out boldly and courageously to stand before the Muslims in the mosque of the Prophet 🌸, proclaiming the truth, urging people and scolding them.

3. The third is the humanitarian factor. Sayyidah al-Zahrā' 🌸 did not go into this battle with weapons or violence. She engaged in this confrontation and battle through rational dialogue based on evidence and proofs that certified the rightfulness of her claims.

The coming together of these factors in Sayyidah al-Zahrā''s 🌸 character in this sermon exemplify the anthropological method. Consider this: Among the basics of the anthropological method is to read history not as past but as something to come, as a way from the past to the future. How to read history as a way from the past to the future? By approaching history through a multidisciplinary approach of social sciences and humanities. Sayyidah al-Zahrā' ﷺ was reading history this way when she said, "'You were on the brink of a pit of Fire'[4]: an easy drink to be had, a ready opportunity for the greedy, and a brand of fire for the person in haste. You were stomped underfoot, drinking rainwater that had been fouled by camels and eating dried meat and leaves; so humiliated and spurned you were, then God saved you through Muḥammad. Through my father Muḥammad, God lit up the darknesses, relieved troubled hearts, and cleared confusion from the eyes, guiding people, saving them from perversity, and making them see after blindness." This was the effect of the Muḥammadan state in that chaotic, *jāhilī* society of infighting. In twenty-three years, the Prophet ﷺ was able to turn it into a superior society in its knowledge, sciences, and aspirations. Sayyidah al-Zahrā' ﷺ also dealt with this society through the anthropological method in her sermon.

The Faith-Based Method

Sayyidah al-Zahrā' ﷺ is a person consumed with God, a person who is from God and to Him ﷻ she shall return. When we view Sayyidah al-Zahrā' ﷺ from this angle, we are reading her through the faith-based method. Sayyidah al-Zahrā' ﷺ engaged in a movement based on the Prophetic message. She ﷺ was not a human being

[4] Sūrat āl-'Imrān, verse 103.

but a movement, a movement of a whole society. She ﷺ experienced the pains and troubles of the message and foretold its future and outcome. When you view Sayyidah al-Zahrā' ﷺ as the driver of the message, she becomes the manifestation of the noble verse: "There has to be a nation among you summoning to the good, bidding what is right, and forbidding what is wrong. It is they who are the felicitous."[5] This means that Sayyidah al-Zahrā' ﷺ exemplifies a faith-based approach that is a role model for every faithful and religious person.

This is the analytical approach that may be humanistic, anthropological, or faith-based.

The Verification Approach

How do we verify history? How do we check its events and prove that they actually happened? When dealing with history we cannot claim absolute certainty; the historical events that we're certain about are numbered. We're certain about the death of Imām al-Ḥusayn ﷺ in that manner, the oppression that Imām 'Alī ﷺ suffered, and the conquest of Mecca. The incidents that inspire certainty are few, so how do we verify the authenticity of other incidents? The first person who attended to the issue of verification using a method of proof is Ibn Khaldūn in his *Muqaddima*. In scientific,

[5] Sūrat Āl 'Imrān, verse 104.

mathematical terms, this proof is called probability. You can analyze history using this proof; it entails gathering the evidence and proofs that indicate that an incident reasonably certainly happened or that its occurrence is more probable than not. This means that using probability to verify history is the scholarly, logical approach. Of course, this approach has several stipulations that we will mention in our examples about Sayyidah al-Zahrāʾ عليها السلام. What are these stipulations?

The first stipulation is that the historical report in question should not be contradicted by a stronger report. An example is the date of Sayyidah al-Zahrāʾ's عليها السلام birth. Concerning the date of Sayyidah al-Zahrāʾ's عليها السلام birth, the famous report among Ahl al-Sunna is that she عليها السلام was born five years before the Prophet's ﷺ mission. This is mentioned by Ibn al-Jawzī in *Tadhkirat al-Khawāṣṣ*, al-Ḥanafī in his *Durar al-Simṭayn*, and al-Ṭabarī in *Dhakhāʾir al-ʿUqbā*. All three authors say that she عليها السلام was born while Quraysh was building up the Sacred House (*al-bayt al-ḥarām*). However, this report cannot be relied upon because it is contradicted by a stronger report among the narrations of Ahl al-Bayt عليهم السلام. After all, Ahl al-Bayt عليهم السلام are more knowledgeable about things that concern them, and their report states that she عليها السلام was born five years after the Prophet's ﷺ mission. How much is the time difference? Based on the first opinion, when Sayyidah al-Zahrāʾ عليها السلام died, she was twenty-eight, whereas according to the second opinion, she was eighteen. It is a big difference of ten years. Later,

I will indicate some of the reasons for the insistence that Sayyidah al-Zahrāʾ was born five years before the Prophetic mission whereas the trustworthy narrations of Ahl al-Bayt state that she was born five years after the mission.

The second stipulation is that the time period when the report was narrated should be chronologically close to the incident. When it comes to the field of history, historians disagree about the century whose narrations may be trusted. Which narrations among those fourteen centuries may be trusted? We read the opinions of some writers about this. Bassām al-Jamal is a Tunisian scholar with a doctoral degree in Arabic Language and Literature. He has written many books, such as *al-Islām al-Sunnī*, *Asbāb al-Nuzūl*, *Laylat al-Qadr fil-Mutakhayyal al-Islāmī*, and *Fāṭimah al-Zahrāʾ Min al-Tārīkh ilā al-Mutakhayyal*. He does not believe in the figure of Sayyidah al-Zahrāʾ, saying that she is exaggerated and that most narrations concerning her are a product of the imagination. He says that we should accept Sayyidah Fāṭima's biographical details in the Sunnī sources from the middle of the third century A.H. all the way back to Ibn Saʿd's *Ṭabaqāt* but no more. The author claims that there are historical incidents related to Sayyidah al-Zahrāʾ, but exaggerations began in the fourth century with al-Ṭabarānī, and certain details began to creep into her biography that can only be accepted out of faith, such as her merits on the Day of Judgment, the order from heaven to for her to be married, or her passing on the Day of Mustering while the people will be told, "Lower your gazes so that Sayyidah Fāṭimah ﷺ the daughter of Muḥammad may pass." According to Bassām al-Jamal, these are all fictions that cannot be accepted. Is this an objective claim?

First of all, there is practically no difference between the mid-third century and the fourth century; it's just a matter of a hundred years. As long as there are trustworthy authors and transmitters, in addition to being not far from the Prophet's time, the transmissions of a given century are reliable. What's the difference between the two centuries, after all? They are both characterized by these two features, and there is no difference between them; they are the same.

Second, the most important thing is the trustworthiness of the material itself. The author is relying on Sunnī sources, but let us consider the narrations of Ahl al-Bayt ﷺ. The narrations of Ahl al-Bayt ﷺ are more trustworthy than those sources that the author deems acceptable. Why do I say that? First, because the narrations of Ahl al-Bayt ﷺ were presented to them for revision; the narrations of Imām al-Bāqir and Imām al-Ṣādiq ﷺ were presented to Imām al-Riḍā ﷺ in writing. Entire written narrations were shown to Imām al-Riḍā ﷺ; he read them, rejected some for being untrue, and accepted others.

This means that the narrations of Ahl al-Bayt ﷺ have been revised; this is one thing. Secondly, the narrations of Ahl al-Bayt ﷺ pre-date the fourth century, going back to the year 229 AH. Third, the members of Ahl al-Bayt ﷺ are more knowledgeable about their own affairs: their history and the history of their ancestors. For this reason, relying on the certified narrations of Ahl al-Bayt ﷺ is the best and most guaranteed choice of action here. We notice that the narrations that he called faith-based were transmitted by Ahl al-Bayt ﷺ, such as that Sayyidah al-Zahrā' ﷺ was married by an order from heaven, or her passing among God's creation on the Day of Mustering, or her many merits. These narrations were not first transmitted by al-Ṭabarānī after the fourth century; they were transmitted a hundred years earlier through Ahl al-Bayt ﷺ and during a reliable historical period.[6]

Third, if we paused at every narration that requires faith, we would have to stop at some of the historical incidents mentioned in the Qur'ān. What did the Qur'ān say about Maryām? "Whenever Zakariyya visited her in the sanctuary, he would find provisions with her. He said, 'O Maryam, from where does this

---

[6] The total lifespan of the Imāms of Ahl al-Bayt ﷺ is 260 years. The lesser occultation (*al-ghayba al-ṣughrā*) ended in 329 A.H., and their legacy was available to the Muslims before the end the third century all the way up to the second half of the fourth century. Their trustworthy companions transmitted their legacy until the fifth century.

come for you?’ She said, ‘It comes from God. God provides whomever He wishes without any reckoning.’”[7] God also tells us that ‘Īsā b. Maryam said, “I will create for you out of clay the form of a bird, then I will breathe into it, and it will become a bird by God’s leave. And I heal the blind and the leper and I revive the dead by God’s leave.”[8] This is also a miraculous touch from the world of the unseen. God even said about the Prophet ﷺ Muḥammad, “Immaculate is He who carried His servant on a journey by night from the Sacred Mosque to the Farthest Mosque whose environs We have blessed, that We might show him some of Our signs.”[9] This means that we can’t just refuse every historical occurrence with an otherworldly touch. The most important thing is to get the report from sound channels according to scholarly standards; then we can accept it even if it has an otherworldly touch. This concludes the second stipulation, which is taking into account the time period that is closest to the incident.

The third stipulation is fame. Some incidents are proved by how famous they are: their narrators and transmitters would be so numerous that the following generation would not have to transmit from the past generation. Each historian would have his own sources;

---

[7] Sūrat āl-‘Imrān, verse 37.

[8] Sūrat āl-‘Imrān, verse 49.

[9] Sūrat al-Isrā’, verse 1.

if the transmitters and narrators are diverse, this inspires certainty about the transmission of the incident. An example is the sermon of Sayyidah al-Zahrā' 🌸; it's a famous sermon among the Sunna and the Shī'a. Many historians and *ḥadīth* transmitters mention this sermon. It was narrated by the following scholars: Aḥmad b. Abī Ṭāhir in *Balāghāt al-Nisā'* since the second century, Abū Bakr al-Jawharī in *al-Saqīfa wa-Fadak*, al-Mas'ūdī's *Murūj al-Dhahab*, al-Khawārizmī from al-Ḥāfiẓ b. Mirdāwayh in his *Maqtal al-Ḥusayn*, Ibn al-Athīr in his *al-Nihāya* and his *Manāl al-Ṭālib* which is about al-'Aqīla Zaynab 🌸, and Ibn Abī al-Ḥadīd in *Sharḥ Nahj al-Balāgha*. All these authors are from our Sunnī brothers. As for Shī'ī authors, there are al-Shaykh al-Ṣadūq in his *'Ilal al-Sharā'i'*, al-Ṭabarī in *Dalā'il al-Imāma*, and al-Irbilī in *Kashf al-Ghumma*. When you see the sheer number of sources narrating the sermon of Sayyidah al-Zahrā' 🌸, you know that it's famous, which makes you certain that the incident actually happened.

The fourth stipulation is that the transmitter of the report should be known for confirming the truth of his reports. If he is a later author who is known for confirming the truth of reports and examining multiple sources, his statements are accepted. An example is Shaykh al-Mufīd's *al-Irshād*. He is a scholar, jurist, and historian who confirms the truth of his reports and insists on using trustworthy sources. For this reason, the statements of Shaykh al-Mufīd are acceptable. In his book, he relates that Sayyidah al-Zahrā' 🌸 came to the

Prophet ﷺ in his final illness and recited: "One fair-faced for whose sake the rain comes down, the refuge of orphans and the stronghold of widows." At that, the Prophet ﷺ opened his eyes and said in a weak voice, "Daughter, that is the saying of your uncle Abū Ṭālib; don't say it. Rather, say, 'Muḥammad is but a prophet ; [other] prophets have passed before him. If he dies or is slain, will you turn back on your heels?'"[10] Sayyidah al-Zahrā' ﷺ cried for a long time, and the Prophet ﷺ gestured for her to come closer. He ﷺ whispered something in her ear that made her face glow with delight. The narration states that Sayyidah Fāṭimah ﷺ was asked, "What did the Prophet whisper to you that it cheered you up so much and made you forget your worry and sadness about his death?" She ﷺ responded, "That I am the first of his household to follow him." This narration was mentioned by Muslim in his *Ṣaḥīḥ*; among our books Shaykh al-Mufīd narrates it in his *al-Irshād* because he is known for confirming the truth of his reports.

The fifth stipulation is that the report should be accompanied by plenty of qualitative proofs that inspire trust in it. An example is doctrinal proofs. If a report does not conform with sound doctrine, we should refuse it. For instance, Bassām al-Jamal refuses the reports about Sayyidah al-Zahrā' ﷺ because they necessitate her infallibility. Some scholars are of the

[10] Sūrat āl-'Imrān, verse 144.

opinion that history should be approached aside from doctrine and projections. However, such an approach does not offer a correct reading of history. For example, it has been stated that the Prophet ﷺ forbade the people of Medina from pollinating the palm trees; they complied, and the palms did not bear fruit that year. Such scholars say that this was the Prophet's ﷺ fault, refusing to use doctrine to approach the issue. Another example is their claim that Imām ʿAlī ؏ married Juwayriyya bt. Abū Jahl while being married to Sayyidah al-Zahrāʾ ؏, which angered both Sayyidah al-Zahrāʾ ؏ and her father ﷺ. However, let us analyze their claim in general and specific terms.

First, the general analysis. Reading history through the doctrine of infallibility is not unobjective; it is reading history from within history itself. It is historically confirmed that the Prophet was at the height of creation based on the text of the Qurʾān: "It is by God's mercy that you are gentle to them; and had you been harsh and hardhearted, surely they would have scattered from around you,"[11] and "and indeed you possess a great character."[12] If we encounter a narration that states that ʿAbd Allāh b. Maktūm came to the Prophet ﷺ to learn the Qurʾān and the Prophet ﷺ turned away, can we accept such a narration? We say that this narration does

---

[11] Sūrat āl-ʿImrān, verse 159.

[12] Surat al-Qalam, 4.

not conform to established history. The same thing applies to infallibility; the infallibility of Ahl al-Bayt constitutes a textually-established historical fact stated in clear Arabic. For this reason, we refuse any narration that does not conform with the concept of infallibility because it contradicts established history. This is not doctrinal projection: "Indeed God desires to repel all impurity from you, O People of the Household, and purify you with a thorough purification."[13] Both Muslim in his *Ṣaḥīḥ* and al-Ḥākim in his *al-Mustadrak* state that the Prophet took hold of Sayyidah Fāṭima, Imām ʿAlī, Imām al-Ḥasan, and Imām al-Ḥusayn and said, "O God, these are the people of my household and my closest relatives: their flesh is my flesh and their blood is my blood." This means that the verse and the established narrations indicate infallibility and purity. Another proof has been mentioned by al-Ḥākim in his *al-Mustadrak*, stating that the Prophet said, "Fāṭimah is a piece of me. God is pleased at her pleasure and is angered at her anger." This statement also indicates infallibility, which means that the concept of infallibility is part of established history.

Secondly, among the proofs used to read history are rational proofs because the judgments of reason are of the basic proofs that are used to read history. For example, when reason rules that God is not a body and is not affected by movement, this is a definitive self-

[13] Surat al-Aḥzāb, verse 33.

evident ruling. Of course, we refuse every narration that contains anthropomorphism (*tajsīm*). In the same way, infallibility is a judgment of reason; Prophethood and Imāmate imply infallibility. This is a result of considering history using rational proofs. Let us now consider the issue of Imām ʿAlī's ؑ engagement to Juwayriyya bt. Abū Jahl. Abū Jahl is one of the Prophet's ﷺ worst enemies. Let's read the narration of al-Miswar b. Makhrama who said that Sayyidah Fāṭimah ؑ came to the Prophet ﷺ and said, "Your people are saying that you do not get angry on your daughters' behalf. ʿAlī ؑ is setting on marrying the daughter of Abū Jahl." The narrator said, "I heard the Prophet recite the *shahāda* and say, 'I made Abū al-ʿĀṣ my son in law and he kept his word to me. Fāṭimah is a piece of me, and I dislike anything that upsets her. By God, the daughter of the Prophet of God and the daughter of the enemy of God will not be wives of the same man.' At that, Imām ʿAlī ؑ gave up the idea of the engagement."

The conclusion of this narration is that Imām ʿAlī ؑ was the one who hurt Sayyidah al-Zahrāʾ ؑ, which makes him included in the Prophet's ﷺ saying, "Fāṭimah is a piece of me. Whoever hurts her hurts me." This narration is rejected both at the level of its chain of transmission and content. Al-Miswar b. Makhrama was in the camp of ʿAbd Allāh b. al-Zubayr, and whenever Muʿāwiya was mentioned in his presence, he sent blessings upon him. In addition, this narration appears in *Tahdhīb al-Tahdhīb*, and Miswar transmits it from Muḥammad b. Shihāb al-Zuhrī, who ultimately transmits it from Imām Zayn al-ʿĀbidīn ﷺ. However, in *Sharḥ Nahj al-Balāgha*, Ibn Abī al-Ḥadīd says that al-Miswar was one of the people who defected from Imām ʿAlī's ﷺ side. Muḥammad b. Shayba said, "I came to Medina and heard Muḥammad b. Shihāb al-Zuhrī and ʿUrwa b. al-Zubayr mentioning ʿAlī and speaking ill of him." For this reason, Ibn Muʿīn discredited the trustworthiness of Muḥammad b. Shihāb al-Zuhrī. Ibn Abī Malīka also narrated this narration; he was a judge appointed by ʿAbd Allāh b. al-Zubayr. This means they all belong to one circle, and their trustworthiness is questionable.[14]

Second of all, al-Miswar himself was born after the second year A.H. Let's assume that Imām ʿAlī ﷺ asked for Juwayriyya's hand in marriage; is this prohibited? Does this contradict the Prophet's ﷺ infallibility? Let's assume, according to the opinion of some scholars, that

---

[14] Several people narrated the engagement of Imām ʿAlī ﷺ to the daughter of Abū Jahl, but the most cited narrator by historians is al-Miswar b. Makhrama from ʿAbd Allāh b. Abī Malīka or Muḥammad b. Shihāb al-Zuhrī from Imām al-Sajjād ﷺ. The lecture discussed their trustworthiness. Some might say that the mention of this engagement exists in Shīʿī sources, and particularly in *ʿIlal al-Sharāʾiʿ*, 1/185. However, the purpose of this narration is to refute the engagement and not to prove it. Some wretched man accused Imām ʿAlī ﷺ of doing so but the Imām ﷺ denied this. In addition, the incident's chain of transmission in Shīʿī sources is weak due to the presence of Aḥmad b. Muḥammad b. Zakariyyā al-Qaṭṭān in it.

taking a second wife to Sayyidah al-Zahrāʾ عليها السلام is prohibited; couldn't the Prophet ﷺ have spoken to Imām ʿAlī عليه السلام before he went up to the pulpit? Doesn't this contradict the character of the Prophet ﷺ: "and is most kind and merciful to the faithful"?[15] Third, how could the Prophet ﷺ call Abū Jahl the enemy of God while he said about Abū al-ʿĀṣ, Juwayriyya's brother, "Welcome him and do not curse his father because cursing the dead hurts the living"? These are the morals of the Prophet ﷺ; how could he get on the pulpit and say such a thing [about Imām ʿAlī عليه السلام?] This narration is questionable in its chain of transmission and content.

The second factor here is social custom. Any report has to be compatible with its social context. In his book, Bassām al-Jamal says about the marriage of Sayyidah al-Zahrāʾ عليها السلام, "I have not found any explicit reasons that explain why none of the young men of Mecca proposed to the daughter of the Prophet of God." In a footnote, he adds, "Maybe Fāṭimah was not beautiful enough for the young men of Quraysh." In other words, he means that the fault is with Sayyidah Fāṭimah عليها السلام herself; this, in his opinion, is consistent with social custom. However, there is no evidence to support the claim that Sayyidah al-Zahrāʾ عليها السلام was over fifteen at the time. We already mentioned that she عليها السلام was born five years after the Prophetic mission. This means she was not married any later than the customary age of the time. Even if we

[15] Sūrat Yūnus, verse 128.

assume that she exceeded fifteen years old but no one proposed to her, this does not mean that she suffered from a fault. Perhaps that was because the Prophet ﷺ and his companions were besieged at Mecca; maybe the companions did not want to propose while under a heavy siege. Why am I focusing on al-Jammāl? He's expressing such despicable ideas. He's not relying on any narration that state that no one proposed to Sayyidah al-Zahrā' ﷺ; he's relying on Ibn al-Jawzī's saying in *Tadhkirat al-Khawāṣṣ* that noblemen and notables proposed to Sayyidah al-Zahrā' ﷺ, such as Abū Bakr, 'Umar, and 'Abd al-Raḥmān b. 'Awf. The Prophet ﷺ used to respond, "I am waiting for the decision" i.e. the command from heaven, which was when the Commander of the Believers proposed.

The third factor is historical possibility. Al-Jammāl also says that Sayyidah al-Zahrā' ﷺ wasn't born five years after the Prophetic mission because Sayyidah Khadīja ﷺ died at sixty-five, ten years after the Prophetic mission. This means that she gave birth to Sayyidah al-Zahrā' ﷺ at sixty, which does not conform to historical antecedents and which affirms that Sayyidah Khadīja ﷺ gave birth to Sayyidah al-Zahrā' ﷺ five years before the Prophetic mission, i.e. at fifty-five years old. However, there is an objection to this claim, which is the following. The author wants to say that Sayyidah Khadīja ﷺ married the Prophet ﷺ at fifty and lived with him for fifteen years, but this is untrue. Sunnī historians say that the Prophet ﷺ married Sayyidah

Khadīja ﷺ when she was between twenty-five and forty-six years old; the range is these two ages. Most Sunnī historians say that the Prophet ﷺ married Sayyidah Khadīja ﷺ when she was twenty-five. This was narrated by al-Bayhaqī and Ibn Kathīr, while al-Balādhurī said that she was forty-six in *Ansāb al-Ashrāf*. Most narrations state that she was twenty-five.

Second, if Sayyidah Khadīja ﷺ was married at fifty, how did the Prophet ﷺ have children? All his children are from Sayyidah Khadīja ﷺ. Al-Qāsim, al-Ṭāhir, and ʿAbdallāh are all Sayyidah Khadīja's ﷺ children. Only Māriya al-Qibṭiyya gave the Prophet ﷺ his son Ibrahīm. Ahl al-Sunna say that Sayyidah Zaynab and Umm Kulthūm were also the Prophet's ﷺ daughters,[16] which means in this case that Sayyidah Khadīja ﷺ gave birth to three daughters and three sons. However, is it historically possible that a woman between fifty and sixty gave birth to six children? Usually, at this age, a woman can no longer have children. I will mention two other examples about historical possibility. Some historians mention that Imām al-Ḥasan ﷺ had ten wives and that he was quick to divorce them such that Imām ʿAlī ﷺ himself said, "Do not give your daughters to my son al-Ḥasan as he has a fondness of divorce." Ibn

[16] There are also Shīʿī scholars who say that Sayyidah Zaynab and Umm Kulthūm ﷺ are the Prophet's ﷺ daughters. This is mentioned in the following sources: Shaykh al-Mufīd, *Ajwibat al-Masā'il al-ʿUkbariyya*, 120, al-Ṭabrisī, *Iʿlām al-Warā*, 146, al-Tustarī, *al-Qāmūs*, 9/450.

Abī al-Ḥadīd reports that some historians said that Imām al-Ḥasan ﷺ married ninety different women. A man who marries this frequently ought to have many children. However, when we count the sons and daughters of Imām al-Ḥasan ﷺ, he had fifteen children. This number does not conform to the claim that he married dozens of wives. The other example is mentioned by al-Ṭabarī. This narration states that when Imām al-Ḥusayn ﷺ departed from Mecca to Iraq and crossed the region of Tanʿīm, he ﷺ saw a caravan of the governor of Yemen, Bujayr b. Yasār, arriving from Yemen. The caravan, which was full of money, goods, and clothes, was the property of Yazīd b. Muʿāwiya. Imām al-Ḥusayn ﷺ confiscated the caravan but let the people associated with it go. Is this a plausible narration? In his *Rijāl*, al-Sayyid Baḥr al-Ulūm rejects this narration. It's true that Imām al-Ḥusayn ﷺ has a mandate over everything, but this narration does not conform to the broader context. Imām al-Ḥusayn ﷺ revolted and said, "I did not revolt out of pride or arrogance." This means that this narration does not conform to the blessed Ḥusaynī movement.

1 Muḥarram, 1443 A.H.

Feminism and Gender
A Critical View

"O mankind! Indeed We created you from a male and a female, and made you nations and tribes that you may identify yourselves with one another. Indeed the noblest of you in the sight of God is the most Godwary among you. Indeed God is all-knowing, all-aware."[17]

There are trends that are influencing the values of Islamic society and invading the Islamic world due to the interaction of Eastern and Western cultures, the exchange of information, and the unchecked openness to Western culture. Of these trends are gender and feminism.

The Difference Between Gender and Feminism

The word gender is an English word of Latin origin. It connotes sex (masculinity and femininity), but it has had different uses with one common factor: the refusal of femininity and masculinity's rootedness in a person. Femininity, according to this view, is not a rooted quality and a definitive characteristic of females. A clarification is available in the *Stanford Encyclopedia of Philosophy*: "'Sex' denotes human females and males depending on biological features (chromosomes, sex organs, hormones and other physical features); 'gender' denotes women and men depending on social factors

[17] Sūrat al-Ḥujurāt, verse 13.

(social role, position, behavior or identity)."[18] According to the feminist movement, gender is a cultural construct; being a man includes women with the behavior of a man. This means that gender acquires its meaning from its social context. As for sex, it is a natural quality. Does gender encompass the spirit of femininity or masculinity? There is no necessary relation between natural qualities and legal and social identities. The latter, in the feminist view, are acquired from natural and social factors. Gender is defined as a feeling, every individual person's feeling of masculinity or femininity as a result of social factors or the social environment. For this reason, feminism has called for the rejection of the differentiation in roles because men and women can do each other's tasks with no difference in their roles.

The feminist movement has begun to invade Arab societies, and particularly the Gulf, making use of the term "gender." Despite feminism's different schools, they all claim that being born a woman does not make someone a woman. In her book *al-Usus al-Falsafiyya lil-Fikr al-Nasawī al-Gharbī*, author Khadīja al-ʿAzīzī says that the feminist movement has several types. One of these types is radical feminism, which calls for abolishing any connection between the sexes. Another type is feminism that focuses on the female's position.

[18] Translator's note: See https://plato.stanford.edu/entries/feminism-gender/#SexDis.

This type states that the female's suffering is due to the role assigned to her within the family.

In her book, *The Second Sex*, French author Simone de Beauvoir says that marriage is a woman's prison because marriage and children kill a woman's ambitions instead of unleashing her creativity and hopes. For this reason, she says that a person is not born a man but becomes a man, and a person is not born a woman but becomes a woman. Man's role of leading the family and the qualities of being a man and a woman are not natural differences but are a result of culture throughout history. Another type is liberal feminism that is widespread among us, which calls for total equality in rights and laws because the difference in roles between men and women is only a social difference. As for radical feminism, it states that man is responsible for woman's backwardness by placing her inside the home, killing her ambitions, and considering her only as someone who raises the children. This means that man is primarily accountable for the restriction and oppression of women. There are two trends: one that abolishes the differences between men and women and therefore a woman's special role as a housekeeper. As a result, this trend destroys the family. The second trend does not reject the differences between men and women but rather calls for equality between the two sides. These movements have destroyed women's humanity. If they are detached from their nurturing role that instills moral values and are thrown in factories in the West to make a living, this deprives them of the role that conforms with their truth and primordial nature.

Feminism's Consequences on Islamic Society

1. Destroying the family: It's obvious that a woman will refuse to marry because she does not want to limit her talents and ambitions.

2. Desecrating motherhood: Motherhood will be considered a marginal, base thing, and being a housekeeper will be considered an uncivilized and a shameful value as that same role may be performed by daycares. For this reason, Mother's Day is beginning to lose its significance all over the world, although many women actually want to become mothers. It is not morally or legally right to push women toward other domains without them being actually convinced of those roles. Freedom of speech means that a woman is able to make the decision that suits her best. It is not right to urge her to leave the family home.

3. Calling for abortion in order to rid women of the consequences and constraints of giving birth.

4. Unleashing sexual freedoms without limit or constraint.

Critiques and Remarks

The feminist movement is based on two pillars:

1. The philosophical pillar: Being a woman is based on her existential status, and the existential status of a woman is the same as that of a man. There is no duality of man and woman; there is one human species that has an intellect, freedom, and will. This means a woman is a conscious, independent, original being that is not subordinate to man or restricted to a certain role. A man can become a woman; this was established by philosopher Simone de Beauvoir who was influenced by her philosopher husband Sartre. Radical feminism made use of this idea, claiming that certain women may live in society without the need for a man and his interference and without any relationship between men and women.

2. The legal pillar: There must be legal similarity and equality between men and women. Liberal feminism made use of this idea in the domains of work and education and in all institutions; it relies on UN documents to defend this idea.

Remarks

The first remark is this: is the difference between men and women simply a difference of organs and hormones or does it also presuppose a difference in positions, roles, and functions? Herein lies the difference between the religious view and the gender-based view. No, the difference is not only physiological but psychological as well. A woman has the capacity for pregnancy, giving birth, breastfeeding, and menstruation, which enforces certain ideas, concepts, and psychological differences between men and women. This is why Jordan Peterson says that the essential differences between men and women cannot be abolished for the sake of equality. A man's emotion toward a woman is different from a woman's emotion toward a man; a woman wants warmth whereas a man needs stability. A man cannot become a mother and a mother cannot become a father. The Qur'ān emphasizes the fact that this difference is natural. It is a difference that complements men and women's psychological and physiological natures, which makes them both need one another: "O mankind! Indeed We created you from a male and a female, and made you nations and tribes that you may identify yourselves with one another. Indeed the noblest of you in the sight of God is the most Godwary among you. Indeed God is all-knowing, all-aware."[19] Human beings differ in their capabilities, including physical strength

[19] Sūrat al-Ḥujurāt, verse 13.

and intelligence; all of this is a complementary difference. This is exactly like the different senses: hearing, sight, and smell. Each of the senses has different capabilities, and each capability represents a complementary difference and not a preferential difference. The Qur'ān states that men and women walk together on this path, that it is a complementary path: "Indeed the Muslim men and the Muslim women, the faithful men and the faithful women, the obedient men and the obedient women, the truthful men and the truthful women, the patient men and the patient women, the humble men and the humble women, the charitable men and the charitable women, the men who fast and the women who fast, the men who guard their private parts and the women who guard, the men who remember God greatly and the women who remember [God greatly] —God holds in store for them forgiveness and a great reward."[20] The difference in roles and positions is due to the difference in capabilities.

The second remark is this. Let us assume that there is no difference. They say that men and women had the same duties but society limited the man to the role of the father and the woman to the role of the mother. The question that arises here is this: at which historical moment was man assigned the role of leading and being strong and woman the role of motherhood and being tender? There is no historical indication that any

[20] Sūrat al-Aḥzāb, verse 35.

transformation took place. If men and women had always been equals, when did their roles differ? This means that human society necessitated different roles from its very beginning based on differences in capabilities and temperaments. It's not true that at a certain point in history, society imposed this difference without taking capabilities and capacities into consideration. There is also a psychological rule in social psychology that states that the more masculine a man is, the more he prefers feminine women and vice versa. This is due to the difference between men and women. A man is not attracted to a manly woman, and a woman is not attracted to a feminine man.

The third remark is this. The author Carol Gilligan had remarks on the propositions of the feminist movement. She said that both men and women are responsible, but what are their motives? A man's perspective on responsibility is different from a woman's. A man always proceeds from the law and establishing justice through his focus on merits and enforcing the law; a man focuses on merit. On the other hand, a woman views responsibility with a focus on morality: selflessness, giving unconditionally, and unlimited sacrifice. A man always considers his rights and her rights from an individualistic perspective, whereas a woman asks, "What has he offered and what has he given?" while she gives unconditionally. The feminist movement says that men and women take equal part in each other's roles, calling for marginalizing moral principles such as selflessness and giving unconditionally. This is basically a call for destroying the family because the family only rests on selflessness and giving unconditionally and not on functionality: "They are a garment for you, and you are a garment for them,"[21] "Do not covet the advantage which God has given some of you over others. To men belongs a share of what they have earned, and to women a share of what they have earned. And ask God for His grace. Indeed God has knowledge of all things."[22]

The Role of Men and Women

According to Islamic Values and Conceptions

Determining values is based on three pillars:

Is there a difference between the purpose behind a woman's existence and a man's existence? The purpose is one; they are both human beings and the Qur'ān focuses on human beings. The purpose of humankind's existence is cultivating the earth and spreading worship upon it: "He brought you forth from the earth and made it your habitation."[23] The purpose is the manifestation of worship and establishing civilization: "Whoever acts righteously, [whether] male or female,

---

21 Sūrat al-Baqara, verse 187.

22 Sūrat al-Nisā', verse 32.

23 Sūrat Hūd, verse 61.

should he be faithful, —We shall revive him with a good life and pay them their reward by the best of what they used to do,"[24] "He brought you forth from the earth and made it your habitation,"[25] "I did not create the jinn and the humans except that they may worship Me."[26] Only the roles are different. A man's role is different from a woman's role.

In legal jurisprudence, for example, there is no absolute law; the law takes social positions into consideration, and social positions are determined by accomplishments. Your accomplishments make you a doctor or a teacher or an engineer. Accomplishments are determined by capabilities and capacities, and since men and women differ in their capacities, they differ in their social positions. For this reason, a man cannot become a mother: "Do not covet the advantage which God has given some of you over others. To men belongs a share of what they have earned, and to women a share of what they have earned. And ask God for His grace. Indeed God has knowledge of all things."[27]

---

[24] Sūrat al-Naḥl, verse 97.

[25] Sūrat Hūd, verse 61.

[26] Sūrat al-Dhāriyāt, verse 56.

[27] Sūrat al-Nisā', verse 32.

The golden rule is equality, but is there a difference in responsibility? They are both responsible for their religious obligations (*taklīf*), but these obligations depend on their capacities. For this reason, the rule of equality is disregarded in the family due to the difference in responsibilities that is due to the difference in capacities.

Does Islam forbid women from working outside the home? The proponents of gender identity say, "Allow a woman to work," but the standard of Islam is different. The standard for the proponents of gender identity is material, i.e. positions and money, whereas the standard of Islam is the message. A man's value in Islam depends on his commitment to the message: "The value of each person is equal to what he does best." A woman's value depends on her religious role and not on her material fortune. Islam honors the religious role of women, with the Qur'ān praising women in their religious roles: "God draws an[other] example for those who have faith: the wife of Pharaoh, when she said, 'My Lord! Build me a home near You in paradise, and deliver me from Pharaoh and his conduct, and deliver me from the wrongdoing lot.' And Mary, daughter of Imran, who guarded the chastity of her womb, so We breathed into it of Our spirit. She confirmed the words of her Lord and His Books, and she was one of the obedient."[28] The

---

[28] Sūrat al-Mulk, verses 11-12.

first of these women is an example in striving and the second is an example in having patience.

The Qur'ān speaks about the woman who was the Prophet's ﷺ partner: "Should anyone argue with you concerning him, after the knowledge that has come to you, say, 'Come! Let us call our sons and your sons, our women and your women, our souls and your souls, then let us pray earnestly and call down God's curse upon the liars.'"[29] In challenging the Christians of Najrān, the Prophet ﷺ highlighted one of the pillars of Islam. When Khadīja is mentioned, the talk is never about her money or her appearance but about her religious role: "She believed in me when the people disbelieved in me, and she sheltered me when the people threw me out, and she gave me my children." Similarly, when the Prophet ﷺ mentions Sayyidah Fāṭimah, he says, "Fāṭimah is a piece of me." For this reason, Sayyidah Fāṭimah had an intimate relationship with her children who remembered her religious role although they lived with her for no more than five or six years. It is narrated that Imām al-Ḥasan said, "I saw my mother Fāṭimah standing in her prayer niche on the eve of Friday. She continued bowing and prostrating until dawn. I heard her praying for the believing men and women by name and supplicating extensively on their behalf without asking for anything for herself. I said to her, 'Mother, why don't you supplicate for yourself as

[29] Sūrat āl-'Imrān, verse 61.

you supplicate for other people?' She said, 'Son, neighbors come before the household.'"

2 Muḥarram, 1443 A.H.

Women's Elevated Position in Islam

"Whoever acts righteously, [whether] male or female, should he be faithful, —We shall revive him with a good life."[30]

Some philosophers scorn the role of women. Rousseau, for instance, said that women's education should revolve around the man, nourishing and feeding him as a child and giving him tranquility as a grownup; this is her role throughout the ages. Another example is Darwin who says that the man surpasses the woman in intellectual endeavors. His proof is that every endeavor that the man engages in would be of better quality than that of the woman, regardless of whether this endeavor required deep thought or not. For this reason, a number of trends and movements called for women's liberation and defending their dignity and rights. These trends and movements are of two types: descriptive and natural.

The Descriptive Movement

The descriptive movement describes reality as it actually is, i.e. a woman is a different entity than a man, and she has not received her rights as he did. To defend women's dignity, this movement calls for giving women these rights. Susan James, who is a neoliberal feminist, belongs to this movement, and she calls for women's rights that are equal to the rights of men.

---

30 Sūrat al-Naḥl, verse 97.

The Natural Movement

The natural movement denies the differences between men and women; physical differences are marginal. Beauvoir, for example, says that societies themselves decided that men may have multiple roles whereas women may only raise the children, and that this is unsound. For her part, Judith Butler denied even natural and sexual differences between the two sexes: a man can be sexually active and the woman passive and the opposite is true. This is a denial of the reality that everyone acknowledges.

Islam does not clash with organizations that call for giving people their rights. Women still suffer from the oppression of men in some Western societies, but that does not mean we cannot go so far that we deny the differences between men and women. Women have a value-based role that influences the creation of culture. In order to understand the role of women, we must approach the topic from three perspectives.

The Philosophical Perspective

God ﷻ is absolute perfection; nothing restricts or limits Him, and He has manifested His essence through beauty (*jamāl*) and majesty (*jalāl*). Might (*quwwa*) and sovereignty (*jabarūt*) are of the attributes of majesty that strike fear in human beings, whereas God's giving, mercy, and sustenance are attributes of beauty. Majesty is "whatever there is in the heavens glorifies God and [whatever there is on] the earth"[31] while beauty is "He who gave everything its creation and then guided it."[32] Both this beauty and majesty have been expressed through His creation. The verse "in all things We have created pairs so that you may take admonition" can be explained in two ways. The first explanation is that since the Big Bang, the universe was made of matter and antimatter. The unity of these two elements created the atom. Even the electron carries its opposite within itself. The second explanation depends on the elements of majesty and beauty: every single creature possesses beauty and majesty. When we contemplate the Qur'ān, we find two hundred verses placing the skies alongside earth: "by the sky and Him who built it, by the earth and Him who spread it."[33] The sky is a building, but not in the meaning endorsed by ancient astronomy: "the sky is a thick existence that nothing can penetrate." When I say the sky is a building, I mean space is filled with stars and planets that follow an unchanging order. The sky is a manifestation of God's majesty.

[31] Sūrat al-Ḥadīd, verse 1.

[32] Sūrat Ṭā Hā, verse 50.

[33] Sūrat al-Shams, verses 5-6.

The earth, on the other hand, is the source of humankind's nourishment and provision: "From it did We create you, into it shall We return you, and from it shall We bring you forth another time,"[34] "He who made the earth for you a cradle, and in it threaded for you ways,"[35] "It is He who made the earth tractable for you; so walk on its flanks and eat of His provision."[36] The earth is a manifestation of God's beauty and the sky is a manifestation of God's majesty: "Surely the creation of the heavens and the earth is more prodigious than the creation of mankind, but most people do not know."[37] A human being also includes the element of beauty and the element of majesty. For example, in God's saying, "those who suppress their anger, and excuse [the faults of] the people, and God loves the virtuous,"[38] suppressing anger is a quality of majesty and power, whereas God's love for the virtuous is an element of beauty.

From this principle masculinity and femininity arose: "By the night when it envelops, by the day when it brightens, by Him who created the male and the

---

[34] Sūrat Ṭā Hā, verse 55.

[35] Sūrat Ṭā Hā, verse 53.

[36] Sūrat al-Mulk, verse 15.

[37] Sūrat Ghāfir, verse 57.

[38] Sūrat āl-ʿImrān, verse 134.

female."[39] This verse is a manifestation of majesty and beauty; the man is God's majesty and the woman, an energy that awakens love, tranquility, and tenderness in the man, is God's beauty. From a philosophical point of view, the woman is a mirror reflecting the beauty of God and the man is a mirror reflecting the majesty of God.

The Qur'ānic Perspective

How did the Qur'ān speak about men and women? Did it consider men superior to women? The Qur'ān actually gave each of them an authentic position. An example is "O mankind! Be wary of your Lord who created you from a single soul, and created its mate from it."[40] This meaning is often repeated in the Qur'ān: "It is He who created you from a single soul, and made from it its mate."[41] There are two explanations for this verse. The first is that the woman was created from man's soul, and the second is that both of them belong to the same kind without one of them being an origin and the other a branch. The verse "There has certainly come to you an prophet from among yourselves"[42]

---

[39] Sūrat al-Layl, verses 1-3.

[40] Sūrat al-Nisā', verse 1.

[41] Sūrat al-A'rāf, verse 189.

[42] Sūrat Yūnus, verse 128.

means a prophet of your kind and not from the angels. Creation from a single soul means creation out of human nature.

Does a person's truth lie in his body or his spirit? The philosophers say that the thingness (*shay'iyya*) of a thing lies in its form and not in its matter. For example, wood is only a raw material that may be used to form a box or a chair or a table. The matter of a person and the thingness of their form is seminal fluid: "Certainly We created man from an extract of clay. Then We made him a drop of [seminal] fluid [lodged] in a secure abode. Then We created the drop of fluid as a clinging mass. Then We created the clinging mass as a fleshy tissue. Then We created the fleshy tissue as bones. Then We clothed the bones with flesh. Then We produced him as [yet] another creature. So blessed is God, the best of creators!"[43] A person's truth is in their spirit. The spirit is the "other creature" mentioned in the previous verse. The human spirit is the form and not the matter of a person. Masculinity and femininity affect a person's character, but they are not qualifications of a person's humanity. A person is made up of three elements: the intellect, the will, and emotions. God also says, "Was he not a drop of emitted semen? Then he became a clinging mass; then He created [him] and proportioned [him], and made of him the two sexes, the male and the

[43] Sūrat al-Mu'minūn, verses 12-14.

female."[44] Scientifically, genes and male chromosomes appear later. The original matter is female. This means that the truth of a person does not lie in their masculinity or femininity; the stage of masculinity and femininity comes after the proportioning stage.

The qualities that lead to a person's excellence or downfall do not involve masculinity and femininity in the Qur'ān. The Qur'ān says that knowledge is not a quality limited to the male or the female. The same applies to willpower: "Whoever desires this transitory life, We expedite for him therein whatever We wish, for whomever We desire. Then We appoint hell for him, to enter it, blameful and spurned"[45] and behavior: "'I do not waste the work of any worker among you, whether male or female; you are all on the same footing,"[46] "Whoever acts righteously, [whether] male or female, should he be faithful, —We shall revive him with a good life."[47] The Qur'ān is telling us that the requirements for advancement and elevation are the same. There are 67 verses that speak of the human being; they focus on the human being without specifying the male or female:

---

[44] Sūrat al-Insān, verses 37-38.

[45] Sūrat al-Isrā', verse 18.

[46] Sūrat āl-'Imrān, verse 195.

[47] Sūrat al-Naḥl, verse 97.

"But *al-insān* is the most disputatious of creatures,"[48] "Rather *al-insān* is a witness to himself,"[49] "*al-Insān* is a creature of haste,"[50] "Indeed We presented the Trust to the heavens and the earth and the mountains, but they refused to bear it, and were apprehensive of it; but *al-insān* undertook it. Indeed he is most unfair and senseless."[51] This proves that males and females are the same in the Qur'ānic view.

The Legal Perspective

What is Islam's perspective about the difference in rights between a man and a woman? Rights, in Islamic legislation, have three pillars:

1. Purposefulness: As faithful people, we consider all of nature purposeful. Everything in the universe has a purpose: "Had there been gods in them other than God, they would surely have fallen apart,"[52] "Soon We shall show them Our signs in the horizons and in their own souls until it becomes clear to them that He is the Real. Is it not sufficient that your

[48] Sūrat al-Kahf, verse 54 (translation changed slightly).

[49] Sūrat al-Qiyāma, verse 14 (translation changed slightly).

[50] Sūrat al-Anbiyā', verse 37 (translation changed slightly).

[51] Sūrat al-Aḥzāb verse 72 (translation changed slightly).

[52] Sūrat al-Anbiyā', verse 22.

Lord is witness to all things?"[53] "In the earth are signs for those who have conviction."[54] This means that the differences that we observe in nature are purposeful differences. What is that purpose? Each two capacities are connected by an action and a reaction; each capacity is entitled to a portion of the other capacity. Let us compare the human being to the earth. The earth is filled with minerals, fortunes, and treasures, and a person has physical and intellectual capacities. There is an action and a reaction between the earth and the human being: "It is He who created for you all that is in the earth."[55] The Prophet ﷺ came and canonized this notion to revive the earth: "Whoever revives a dead plot of earth becomes its owner." We apply this legal analogy to men and women: men have capacities and women have capacities, and the Qur'ān establishes the following law between them: "they are a garment for you, and you are a garment for them."[56]

2. The philosophers say that a human being has two kinds of existence: existence in itself and existence

---

[53] Sūrat Fuṣṣilat, verse 53.

[54] Sūrat al-Dhāriyāt, verse 20.

[55] Sūrat al-Baqara, verse 29.

[56] Sūrat al-Baqara, verse 187.

for itself. Existence in itself is the intellectual or physical capacities within a person's character, while existence for itself uses existence in itself to fulfill a future act. Human beings have been given knowledge: "taught *al-insān* what he did not know,"[57] an intellect: "who listen to the word [of God] and follow the best [sense] of it. They are the ones whom God has guided, and it is they who possess intellect,"[58] and a will: "and that nothing belongs to *al-insān* except what he strives for."[59] These three elements constitute existence for itself, a practical future investment.

3. Qualitative and not quantitative equality: If we just said that both men and women possess the three human elements of intellect, ability, and will, why don't they have equal rights like neoliberal feminism and other movements want? There is a difference between qualitative and quantitative equality. An example is this. Let's suppose that a father wanted to divide up his will before his death. Some might tell him, "Divide your will equally in everything." However, such a division is not fair. A sound division depends on capacities: "Certainly We sent Our apostles with manifest proofs, and We sent

[57] Sūrat al-'Alaq, verse 5.

[58] Sūrat al-Zumar, verse 18.

[59] Sūrat al-Najm, verse 39.

down with them the Book and the Balance, so that mankind may maintain justice."[60] Distributing the fortune equally is not maintaining justice. The same applies to men and women. God did not equate them quantitatively but qualitatively. It's the value of the right that matters, and equality in humanity led to qualitative equality.

4. The unity of purpose despite the multiplicity of mechanisms and methods: The general purpose of the lawgiver is nurturing three relationships: the relationship of a person to God, the relationship of a person to nature, and the relationship of a person to society. The purpose of the Sharia is to manifest these relationships: "Certainly, the faithful have attained salvation —those who are humble in their prayers, who avoid vain talk, who carry out their [duty of] *zakāt*, who guard their private parts,"[61] "He who created death and life that He may test you [to see] which of you is best in conduct."[62] Everything has a purpose. Fasting has a purpose: "O you who have faith! Prescribed for you is fasting as it was prescribed for those who were before you, so that you may be Godwary." The same applies to prayer, usury, and oppression. Every legislation has

---

[60] Sūrat al-Ḥadīd, verse 25.

[61] Sūrat al-Mu'minūn, verses 1-5.

[62] Sūrat al-Mulk, verse 2.

general and specific purposes. All these purposes are common to men and women, but their method of application is different. The woman who raises the children has her own method in nurturing them. Another example is the verse: "Prepare against them whatever you can of power."[63] The kind of power differs across different times. In our time, we need scientific power. Even Ahl al-Bayt ﷺ had one purpose but a variety of roles. Their purpose was to establish justice and revive the statement of "there is no god but God." This is why the Prophet ﷺ says, "These two sons of mine are Imāms no matter what."

3 Muḥarram, 1443 A.H.

---

[63] Sūrat al-Anfāl, verse 60.

The Biological Differences and Complementary Relationship Between the Sexes

"But the faithful, men and women, are comrades of one another: they bid what is right and forbid what is wrong and maintain the prayer, give the zakāt, and obey God and His Prophet . It is they to whom God will soon grant His mercy. Indeed God is all-mighty, all-wise."[64]

Dr. Alice Rossi, a sociologist, stated that anyone who denies the differences between men and women is actually contradicting the sciences of biology and neurology. Denying these differences is like denying the weather or the existence of the Himalayas. The new developments of birth control, surrogacy, in vitro fertilization (IVF), and contraceptives cannot erase the differences between the sexes because these differences run much deeper. The differences are in the brain's structure and priorities, and not in the ability to become pregnant and give birth. Our discussion is about the comparison between the gender movement and religious thought. The gender movement erases and denies the differences whereas religious thought assigns roles based on nature. There are two points of disagreement between the two camps:

1. There are natural differences that everyone admits, but should rights be based on these differences or

[64] Sūrat al-Tawba, verse 71.

should they be based on equality regardless of these differences?

2. At the level of the family, is the relationship between the man and the woman like a job or a legal form or is this relationship complementary and based on ethical treatment?

Establishing the differences between men and women is discussed at three levels.

The Fixed Differences Between Men and Women

Are the differences between the sexes marginal, as the gender movement claims? In other words, are the differences limited to the reproductive organs or do they actually affect the system of rights? We say that the difference is at three levels.

1. The biological difference in the structure of the brain: In his book (p. 268), *al-Mukhkh: Dhakar Am Unthā?*, author ʿAmr Sharīf mentions that there are differences between men and women. He says that every human being has two sides in their brain: an analytical, deductive side and an emotional, imaginative, intuitive, creative side. The right side is responsible for intuition, creativity, and the imagination while the left side is responsible for analysis and deductions. Men are better in categorical intelligence, i.e. categorizing things and

classifying them, while women are better in linguistic and social intelligence. In the case of children, girls are better at getting along with others and expressing themselves linguistically whereas boys are better at categorical intelligence. The other difference is this. In the case of the male, his intellectual functions are somewhat separate and compartmentalized. In the woman's case, the left hemisphere that is responsible for analysis has a deeper connection to the right hemisphere. The third difference is that if you present the same problem to a man and a woman who belong to the same profession, both being doctors for example, the man directly tackles the basics of the problem and disregards the details. This is why he has what is called a strategic brain. The woman, in contrast, approaches the problem with its specific details, and this is why she has what is called an executive brain.

2. The psychological difference, which has five aspects:

    a. In the same book (p. 208), Dr. ʿAmr Sharīf says that a study was conducted on men and women from six modern societies. The question was, "Who do you want to be and what are your priorities?" The answer of the men was, "I want to be an important person with money, influence, and power." The women said they wanted to be "liked and giving and wanted to contribute to helping others." A man's priorities are economic and political, and he's always thinking about how to make a fortune. A woman's priorities center around social and humanitarian projects.

b. David Buss conducted a study on ten thousand women from thirty-eight different cultures asking them about the characteristics that they look for in a man. A woman focuses on the man's professional and social status because the most important quality for her is safety whereas the man focuses on physical aspects because they grant him love, tranquility, and pleasure.

c. Empathy: "O mankind! Indeed We created you from a male and a female, and made you nations and tribes that you may identify yourselves with one another. Indeed the noblest of you in the sight of God is the most Godwary among you."[65] Identification among people is part of empathy. In social psychology, there is something called the empathy scale. Can you read another person's facial expressions before they speak? Are they confused, optimistic, or pessimistic? Robert Rogan conducted a study on six thousand people and reached the conclusion that a person who is able to read

[65] Sūrat al-Ḥujurāt, verse 13.

facial expressions is better at social adaptation. It has been proven that a woman is more capable than a man in reading facial expressions. For this reason, a wife understands her husband just from looking at his face better than her husband understands her from looking at her face. This makes a woman qualified to be a mother; she needs to read the baby's face to know how he's doing, particularly in the baby's first years.

d. The standard of success: the standard of success for men is advancing up the professional ladder, with the accompanying increase in fortune and influence. This is success. A woman's standard of success is based on how much people like her and how much her social status increases. A man looks at his business partner as a competitor at the professional level, whereas a woman is cooperative with her colleagues. This means a man is prepared to sacrifice money and friends to climb up the professional ladder, whereas a woman finds it difficult to sacrifice her social spirit.

e. How does a person deal with stress? They go through three stages of alarm, resistance, and exhaustion. Men and women are the same at the alarm and resistance stage. However, when a woman reaches the third stage, her estrogen levels go up, and she backs down and relaxes. This could lead to depression and compulsions. When a man reaches the third stage, his testosterone levels go up, and he becomes more aggressive.

3. The Behavioral Difference:

   a. Women tend to choose careers that involve communication with others rather than individualistic careers. Examples are education, medicine, nursing, and psychology. A woman is not inclined to professions such as business, industry, trade, and transportation and shipping. These four careers naturally don't appeal to women even if they are actually employed in them.

   b. How do men and women run a company? A woman runs her employees and company with the spirit of motherhood. Successful women executives state that they run their companies like they run their homes, that is, with compassion but without excess that leads to administrative corruption. Women do not sternly monitor their employees but rather they give them positive reinforcement. A male executive deals with his employees with the sternness of the law.

c. How does a man view the family and how does a woman view it? The family is one of the man's institutions. Perhaps he cares about his profession more than he cares about his family. As for the woman, the family is her primary institution and not just one institution among many.

Differences Between Religious and Gender-Based Trends

There are three questions to be answered:

1. Is the biological background definitive? In other words, are these differences permanent or are they based on capacity? For example, if a person comes from a family of intelligent people, will they necessarily be smart? This person has the capacity to be smart but it isn't inevitable. Personal backgrounds are the same: a person born in a faithful home may deviate. Prior conditions only create a capacity. Are all men different from all women? No. A woman may have an analytical intellect and leadership qualities, and a man may be emotional in his thought process. Males and females as sexes have differences among them, but these differences are not definitive.

2. How do we deal with these differences? Do we ignore them or do we use them to establish a system of rights upon them? The answer was given by American journalist Aline Wheeler who struggled alongside feminist movements for forty-one years, calling for absolute equality between men and women. Later, she discovered that she was living a lie and that certain kinds of men push women to act like that. The differences between men and women became as clear as day to her. For this reason, she calls for approaching the differences from a complementary perspective based on sharing and taking advantage of these differences. The relationship between a man and a woman has to be a relationship of connection and not competition and independence.

3. How do we formulate the relationship between men and women given these differences? Is it a relationship of independence? Can women participate in all domains? A woman would say yes. Thatcher was the British Prime Minister for years, Merkel has been the chancellor of Germany, and there was Bilqīs in the age of Prophet Sulaymān ﵇. This means women are not incapable. However, does women's work in all domains preserve their creative and innovative abilities?

Complementary and Innate Differences

First, we will go over the theory of independence that the feminist movement proposes. Both men and women are conscious, independent human beings, so why shouldn't a woman go into professional domains as long as she has all the required capacities? A Kuwaiti author wrote an article entitled, "Give Us Women A Chance!" Civilizations throughout history gave men a chance, so why not do the same with women? We answer her based on the answer of the famous psychologist Jordan Peterson:

Twenty-five years ago, a statistical, psychological study was conducted on different samples out of fifty-five different peoples. It was a study of character traits: neuroticism, extraversion, openness, agreeableness, and conscientiousness. The result was that as equality increases between men and women, they grow further apart psychologically and behaviorally. The more competitive they are forced to be, the bigger the gap between them. Scandinavian countries, particularly Denmark and Sweden, enforce a very strict equality. The consequence was that the differences between the two sides increased and women became anxious and tense as a result of the competition. In Somalia, which does not enforce laws of equality, there is a greater psychological closeness and compatibility. These studies were mentioned in the journal *Science* and the famous *Time Magazine*.

There is a cultural difference and a psychological difference. If we tell men and women that they are equal and that there is no difference between them, the psychological difference between them increases. The more we decrease the cultural difference, the greater the psychological difference becomes, which makes the establishment of the family harder.

What is the purpose of calling for equality in all positions? It's good for a person to have as much freedom and ability to decide as they desire. However, when a woman becomes open to all professional domains, this will be at the expense of two things. The first is her own child who will lose the chance of a safe, stable, happy life. This comes at the expense of the child who we had hoped would be productive. The second thing is that this makes a woman tenser and more anxious than she was before she entered into those domains. The West has been attempting this for about two-hundred years. Look at the West and the result of these attempts in the West.

The Religious Theory

Religion says, "I acknowledge the psychological differences between the two sides. I distribute rights and roles based on this natural difference between men and women."

Purposefulness: The difference between men and women is a part of the design of the universe; it is a purposeful design. If we go back to the Qur'ān, God says, "O mankind! Indeed We created you from a male and a female, and made you nations and tribes that you may identify yourselves with one another."[66] Since there are differences, men and women should have jobs and rights that are based on those differences. The relationship between men and women is complementary. The difference is caused by purposeful design: "Of His signs is that He created you from dust, then, behold, you are humans scattering [all over]! And of His signs is that He created for you mates from your own selves that you may take comfort in them, and He ordained affection and mercy between you. There are indeed signs in that for a people who reflect. Among His signs is the creation of the heavens and the earth, and the difference of your languages and colors. There

[66] Sūrat al-Ḥujurāt, verse 13.

are indeed signs in that for those who know."[67] Just as the design of the heavens and the earth is purposeful, so is the complementary relationship between men and women.

Shahīd Muṭahharī's Theory on Women's Rights

Shahīd Muṭahharī says that the roles of men and women are different only within the family. Outside the family, men and women are equal and there is no difference among them.

The Theory of ʿAllāma Ṭabāṭabāʾī

ʿAllāma Ṭabāṭabāʾī says that men and women perform their roles and competences in a different way. However, differentiating between things inside and outside the family is illogical.

To repeat, religion does not forbid women from entering different domains as long as that doesn't lead to committing prohibited acts and engaging in illicit relationships. A woman may work in any domain, but can she excel in any domain? That is the question. The difference in the natures of men and women makes each of them excel in different places. We call for qualitative and not quantitative equality where both men and women excel based on their capacities and capabilities.

[67] Sūrat al-Rūm, verse 20.

One of the stipulations is that the woman should be a mother and excel in this domain. Both the woman and the man form the structure of the family. In a happy family, a father and a mother give birth to generous sons and daughters. After all, Sayyidah Fāṭimah ﷺ nurtured male youths and men and taught them to excel on the path of al-Ḥusayn ﷺ.

4 Muḥarram, 1443 A.H.

Intellectual Heritage in Sayyidah Fāṭima's ﷺ Sermon

"This is an explanation for mankind, and a guidance and advice for the Godwary."

One of the best and most beautiful sermons that reached us from Ahl al-Bayt ﷺ is the Fadak Sermon of Sayyidah al-Zahrāʾ ﷺ.

We will discuss three dimensions: the philosophy of religion in the sermon, its principles, and the purposes of the Sharia mentioned in it.

The Philosophy of Religion

What is religion? What is the Sharia? What is the philosophy of religion and what are its dimensions? Religion is the kind of thought that answers four questions that occur naturally to people: "Where did I come from? Where am I going? What is my trajectory? What's the purpose of my existence?" All the heavenly religions attempt to answer these questions. Where did I come from? "Were they created from nothing? Or are they [their own] creators?"[68] Where am I going? "Then We created the drop of fluid as a clinging mass. Then We created the clinging mass as a fleshy tissue. Then We created the fleshy tissue as bones. Then We clothed the bones with flesh. Then We produced him as [yet] another creature. So blessed is God, the best of creators!

---

[68] Sūrat al-Ṭūr, verse 35.

Then indeed you die after that. Then you will indeed be raised up on the Day of Resurrection."[69] What is my trajectory? "O man! You are laboring toward your Lord laboriously, and you will encounter Him;"[70] and the link between the beginning and the end is: "I did not create the jinn and the humans except that they may worship Me."[71] What's the purpose of my existence? "Blessed is He in whose hands is all sovereignty, and He has power over all things. He, who created death and life that He may test you [to see] which of you is best in conduct. And He is the All-mighty, the All-forgiving."[72]

The Sharia is different. It's not the same as the term religion; it does not encompass all religious laws: "He has prescribed for you the religion which He had enjoined upon Noah and which We have [also] revealed to you, and which We had enjoined upon Abraham, Moses and Jesus, declaring, 'Maintain the religion, and do not be divided in it,'"[73] "For each [community] among you We had appointed a code [of law] and a

---

[69] Sūrat al-Mu'minūn, verses 14-16.

[70] Sūrat al-Inshiqāq, verse 6.

[71] Sūrat al-Dhāriyāt, verse 56.

[72] Sūrat al-Mulk, verses 1-2.

[73] Sūrat al-Shūra, verse 13.

path."[74] What is the Sharia? The Sharia is based on four pillars:

1. Doctrine: such as monotheism, prophethood, justice, Imāmate, and the Day of Return.

2. Laws, be they specific or general.

3. Rights which codify the relationship between people. For example, if we say that maintenance (*nafaqa*) is required of the husband, this makes it a code of law from the husband's perspective and a right from the wife's perspective. A wife's maintenance is a debt that the husband owes her. If he dies, the cost of maintenance is taken from the inheritance he leaves behind.

4. Ethics which are the values and ideals that constitute the perfect character. They include justice, humility, and suppressing anger. There are no penal codes associated with ethics, but there are penal codes associated with the law. Breaking the law has a certain punishment, but there is no punishment for arrogance.

---

[74] Sūrat al-Mā'ida, verse 48.

What is the Philosophy of Religion?

There is a difference between the science of philosophy and philosophy. The science of philosophy discusses existence as an existent (*al-wujūd bi mā huwā mawjūd*). In contrast, philosophy itself is an analytical reading of things, such as asking what is the philosophy of language? Where did language come from and what are its purposes? The same applies to the philosophy of religion: how did religion arise and what are its effects on society? All of these questions belong to the philosophy of religion.

The Dimensions of the Philosophy of Religion

The historical dimension: when did religion begin on the face of this earth? Let's go back to archeology. Archeology shows us evidence of religious rites, and science proves that religion existed with the very first human being and from the appearance of human beings on earth. Concerning prayer, God tells us that Prophet ʿĪsā ﷺ said, "He has made me blessed, wherever I may be, and He has enjoined me to [maintain] the prayer and to [pay] the *zakāt* as long as I live."[75] This means that prayer was part of Prophet ʿĪsā's ﷺ religious law; the *zakāt* also existed in all religious laws. Another example is that Muslim jurists say that the blood money for unintentional killing is one hundred red camels.

[75] Sūrat Maryam, verse 31.

However, who established this law? It was 'Abd al-Muṭṭalib, the Prophet's ﷺ grandfather.

The complementary dimension: What is the relationship between laws, rights, and ethics? The relationship is complementary. For instance, God ﷻ says, "There is life for you in retribution, O you who possess intellects! Maybe you will be Godwary!"[76] "And whoever is killed wrongfully, We have certainly given his heir an authority."[77] These are laws. At another level, God speaks about ethics: "But if one is granted any extenuation by his brother, let the follow up [for the blood-money] be honorable, and let the payment to him be with kindness."[78] This also applies to marital relations: the verse "then [let there be] either an honorable retention, or a kindly release" is the law and the verse "and if you fear a split between the two of them, then appoint an arbiter from his relatives and an arbiter from her relatives. If they desire reconcilement, God shall reconcile them"[79] is the ethical dimension. This combination of ethics and the law shows us that religion is made up of these interrelated dimensions.

---

[76] Sūrat al-Baqara, verse 179.

[77] Sūrat al-Isrā', verse 33.

[78] Sūrat al-Baqara, verse 178.

[79] Sūrat al-Nisā', verse 35.

The social dimension: Many religious rulings have social aspects. The *khums*, communal prayers, attending funeral processions, and commanding the right and forbidding the wrong all have social aspects. What is the influence of this dimension? If a man was killed intentionally and his guardian has given up his right for punishment, some jurists do not drop this right entirely because the social right remains. Even wielding a weapon is considered a social crime by some jurists.

The analytical dimension: there are four manifestations of the analytical dimension of religion. Shahīd Sayyid Muḥammad Bāqir al-Ṣadr ﵀ mentions these four concepts in his book, *Iqtiṣāduna*.

1. The purposes (goals) of religion: In addition to answering the four questions mentioned earlier, the purpose of religion is to connect this world to the Hereafter. The Qur'ān refers to this connection: "Whoever desires this transitory life, We expedite for him therein whatever We wish, for whomever We desire. Then We appoint hell for him, to enter it, blameful and spurned. Whoever desires the Hereafter and strives for it with an endeavor worthy of it, should he be faithful —the endeavor of such will be well-appreciated."[80]

[80] Sūrat al-Isrā', verses 18-19.

2. The purposes of the Sharia: They are the lofty goals considered by the Sharia in regards to organizing the three relationships of a person with God, nature, and society. The relationship to heaven is the spiritual element: "And maintain the prayer for My remembrance."[81] Since the second relationship is with nature, you must have a vital role in reviving the earth and civilization: "He brought you forth from the earth and made it your habitation."[82] The third relationship is with society: "and ill feeling for a people should never lead you to be unfair. Be fair; that is nearer to God-wariness, and be wary of God. God is indeed well aware of what you do."[83]

3. The regulations: They are the general guidelines of the Sharia. The rulings of banks and inheritances all fall under the economic branch of Islam, which is a general guideline. The relationships with one's parents, neighbors, and relatives constitute the social branch, and punishments belong to the penal branch of Islam.

4. The reasoning: God ﷻ did not legislate rulings haphazardly. Imām al-Ṣādiq ﷺ says something with the following meaning: "God did not prohibit wine

[81] Sūrat Ṭā Hā, verse 14.

[82] Sūrat Hūd, verse 61.

[83] Sūrat al-Mā'ida, verse 8.

> for its name but for its consequences. Anything that has the consequences of wine is considered wine." This is called the cause or reasoning of a ruling. The reasoning of prayer is: "Indeed the prayer prevents indecencies and wrongs."[84] The reasoning of the ruling on usury is: "O you who have faith! Be wary of God, and abandon [all claims to] what remains of usury, should you be faithful. And if you do not, then be informed of a war from God and His Prophet. And if you repent, then you will have your principal, neither harming others, nor suffering harm."[85] This means that the reasoning is to prevent harm.

The Principles in the Fadak Sermon

The sermon addressed the quality of being chosen: "Know that I am Fāṭimah and that my father is Muḥammad. I speak first and last, and I do not speak in error, nor do I act out of injustice. 'There has certainly come to you a Prophet from among yourselves. Grievous to him is your distress; he has deep concern for you, and is most kind and merciful to the faithful.'[86] If you consider his heritage and know him, you will find that he is my father alone out of all of your women and

---

[84] Sūrat al-'Ankabūt, verse 45.

[85] Sūrat al-Baqara, verses 278-279.

[86] Sūrat al-Tawba, verse 128.

the brother of my cousin alone out of all your men. Blessed be the relation to him." It is as though Sayyidah Fāṭimah ﷺ is referring to the verse: "Indeed God chose Adam and Noah, and the progeny of Abraham and the progeny of Imran above all the nations; some of them are descendants of the others, and God is all-hearing, all-knowing."[87] She also spoke about the history of prophethood: "He [God] saw the nations as factions in their religions, adoring fires and worshiping idols, denying God, though they know Him. Through my father Muḥammad, God lit up the darknesses, relieved troubled hearts, and cleared confusion from the eyes."

Later, she ﷺ said, "My father diverged from the path of the polytheists, striking them squarely and snuffing out their breaths... Whenever polytheistic plots bared their teeth, he threw his cousin into their jaws. The latter did not turn back until he trod on these plots with the soles of his feet and extinguished their flames with his sword, striving in God's way and struggling for the sake of His command. In this, he was close to the Prophet of God ﷺ, the master of the Friends of God, raising his garments in his efforts, and diligently toiling. Meanwhile, you were living the life of luxury in peace, pleasure, and safety as you plotted against us." Here she ﷺ spoke of the radiant history of her father and husband ﷺ.

[87] Sūrat āl-'Imrān, verses 33-34.

Sayyidah Fāṭimah ﷺ also attended to the issue of Fadak. She said, "Did you intentionally abandon the Book of God and leave it behind? God says, 'Solomon inherited from David.'[88] In the story of Yaḥyā b. Zakariyyā ﷺ, God tells us of when Zakariyyā ﷺ said to his Lord, 'grant me from Yourself an heir who may inherit from me and inherit from the House of Jacob.'[89] God also said, 'But the blood relatives are more entitled to inherit from one another in the Book of God'[90] and 'God enjoins you concerning your children: for the male shall be the like of the share of two females,[91]' and 'when death approaches any of you and he leaves behind any property, is that he makes a bequest for his parents and relatives in an honorable manner, —an obligation on the Godwary.'[92] After all this, you claim that I am entitled to nothing and that I do not inherit from my father because we are not womb relatives? Did God designate a verse for you that he excluded my father from? Or is your justification that the people of two different religions do not inherit from one another and that my father and I belong to two different religions?

---

[88] Sūrat al-Naml, verse 16.

[89] Sūrat Maryam, verse 6.

[90] Sūrat al-Anfāl, verse 75.

[91] Sūrat al-Nisā', verse 11.

[92] Sūrat al-Baqara, verse 180.

Or is it that you know the Qur'ān better than my father and cousin?"

The Doctrinal Content

In her sermon, Sayyidah Fāṭimah ﷺ spoke of the five principles of religion: monotheism, prophethood, justice, Imāmate, and the Day of Return. She ﷺ said, "I testify that there is no god but God alone and that He has no partner. It is a phrase that is explained by sincerity. God established the message of this phrase in the hearts and lit up the comprehensible portion of it in the minds. He is the one whom sights cannot see, tongues cannot describe, and illusions cannot explain." The Qur'ān features the words *wāḥid* and *aḥad*. What is the difference between them? "Say, 'I am just a human being like you. It has been revealed to me that your God is the One God [*ilāhun wāḥid*],"[93] "Say, 'He is God, the One [*aḥad*].'"[94]

The Second Principle of Faith

Absolute perfection belongs to God ﷻ. If a person comes to know the oneness of *wāḥidiyya* and *aḥadiyya*, they believe that God ﷻ is absolute perfection. However, absolute perfection has manifestations; of

[93] Sūrat al-Kahf, verse 110.

[94] Sūrat al-Ikhlāṣ, verse 1.

these manifestations are richness, wisdom, and justice. Sayyidah Fāṭimah عليها السلام said, "He [God] originated all things from nothing, and formed them without relying on other examples. He brought them into being with His power and created them with His will although He does not need to create them and does not benefit from forming them." This is a reference to God's richness. She عليها السلام continued, "He only did so to establish His wisdom, raise attention about obeying Him, and demonstrate His power." This is a reference to divine wisdom. Afterward, Sayyidah Fāṭimah عليها السلام said, "He prescribed rewards for obeying Him and established punishments for disobeying Him." This is a reference to justice. "He did so to keep His servants away from His wrath and to lead them to heaven." This is a reference to mercy.

Prophethood

"I testify that my father Muḥammad is God's servant and messenger. He chose him and selected him before He sent him as a messenger, and He named him before He selected him. He chose him before giving him his prophetic mission when all creatures were still hidden in the world of the unseen, guarded by the veils of awe and connected to the ends of nothingness. Sayyidah Fāṭimah عليها السلام wanted to say that her father ﷺ went through four stages: being chosen, named, selected, and sent. God ﷻ chose the Prophet ﷺ and elected him ﷺ before sending him. Like the poet said,

"God searched the East and the West, selecting the essence of Aḥmad over the rest.

He did not become the noblest of prophets until God knew he was the purest."

God ﷻ chose and elected Muḥammad ﷺ using the truth of light. "And He taught Adam the Names, all of them."[95] Did Adam ﷺ use a language to speak the names to the angels? No, there were truths of light that Adam ﷺ saw; the names were made of light that became manifest to Adam ﷺ. These truths of light are Muḥammad and his family ﷺ. The Prophet ﷺ was named before this light came into being. One light was of the Prophet Muḥammad ﷺ, one was of Imām ʿAlī ﷺ, and so on. God ﷻ chose the Prophet ﷺ and elected him ﷺ before sending him. Actual prophethood lies in the fact that the Prophet Muḥammad ﷺ was born, and forty years later, he was sent on his mission: "It is He who sent to the unlettered [people] an apostle from among themselves, to recite to them His signs, to purify them."[96]

---

[95] Sūrat al-Baqara, verse 31.

[96] Sūrat al-Jumuʿa, verse 2.

Imāmate

Sayyidah Fāṭimah 🌸 said, "It was a pledge offered to you, and a remnant of over you." Imāmate is a pledge: "And when his Lord tested Abraham with certain words, and he fulfilled them, He said, 'I am making you the Imām of mankind.' Said he, 'And from among my descendants?' He said, 'My pledge does not extend to the unjust.'"[97] "It is a pledge offered to you and a remnant of vicegerency over you." This is a reference to the Book of God and the pure family of the Prophet 🌸.

The Day of Return

"The best judge is God, the leader is Muḥammad, and the date is the Resurrection. When the Hour comes, you will lose much, and your regrets will not avail you: "Soon you will know whom a disgraceful punishment will overtake and on whom a lasting punishment will descend.'"[98]

The Sermon and the Purposes of the Sharia

There are four aspects of the Sharia's purposes in this great sermon. The sermon divides legislation into legislation of the body (*tashrīʿ jawāriḥī*) and the heart

---

[97] Sūrat al-Baqara, verse 124.

[98] Sūrat Hūd, verse 39.

(*tashrīʿ jawāniḥī*), with individual and social functions. Sayyidah Fāṭimah ﷺ said, "He instituted faith to cleanse you of polytheism and patience to help you earn reward." Both of these are instances of worship related to the heart. She ﷺ continued, "He instituted prayer to raise you above arrogance and fasting to confirm your sincerity." There are general acts of worship and there are specific physical acts of worship: "He instituted *zakāt* to purify your souls and increase your sustenance, and the pilgrimage to establish your religion." These are general acts of worship. Sayyidah Fāṭima's ﷺ sermon also divided functions into individual and social ones: "Wine was forbidden to raise people above impurities, and stealing was prohibited to reinforce chastity." These are individual functions. "*Jihād* is the glory of Islam, and commanding the good sets the affairs of the public straight." These are general functions.

There is a difference between the reason and the wisdom of a ruling. The reason is the domain that revolves around legislation and is interconnected to it. As for the wisdom, it means the applicable benefits. An example is this. What is the reason for prohibiting wine? The reason is that it causes intoxication. The reason for prohibiting usury is that it involves harm: "O you who have faith! Be wary of God, and abandon [all claims to] what remains of usury, should you be faithful. And if you do not, then be informed of a war from God and His apostle. And if you repent, then you will have your principal, neither harming others, nor suffering harm."[99] Do not harm others or suffer harm yourself. The divorced woman waits for three periods of purity: "Divorced women shall wait by themselves for three periods of purity [after menses]."[100] Some narrations state that this is to prevent the mixing up of seminal fluids and lineages. However, even if this woman did not have intercourse with her husband for a whole year before the divorce, she still has to wait. This means that the waiting period is a benefit and not a reason in itself. Another example is *zakāt*. *Zakāt* purifies the soul; this is the reason behind it. As for the increase in sustenance that it entails, it is only a benefit.

Islamic legislations are of two types: constant legislations and variable legislations. For example, returning *salāms* is an obligation, but if it creates difficulty, this ruling is no longer valid. Similarly, if fasting is harmful and difficult, its ruling is no longer valid. These are variable rulings. As for killing a soul or violating others' honor, they are never justified and the prohibition on them is constant. If a person cannot find water or earth [to purify themselves for prayer], the obligation of prayer is no longer valid according to some jurists. This person may still be required to fulfill their missed prayers.

---

[99] Sūrat al-Baqara, verses 278-279.

[100] Sūrat al-Baqara, verse 228.

Constant rulings are related to the structure of religion or to the stability of social life: "and the pilgrimage to establish your religion." The pilgrimage is obligatory in all cases. The sound narration of Mu'āwiya b. 'Ammār from Imām al-Ṣādiq ﷺ states the following: "If the people abandon the pilgrimage, the governor should force them to perform it while he takes care of their expenses." The Ka'ba should never be empty of pilgrims; if they are poor, the governor should spend money from the treasury to sustain them. Justice is another constant ruling: "He enjoined justice to spread harmony among people's hearts."

How do we discover the reason for a ruling? It is mentioned that Imām al-Ṣādiq ﷺ said that religion cannot be determined by deficient intellects or corrupt opinions, so how can we determine the reasons? The first way is the textual, i.e. by the existence of a narration that explains the reason for the ruling. "God ordered those who wash the dead to perform major ablution (*ghusl*) to purify themselves of the fumes of the dead. When the spirit leaves a person's body, they spread disease more easily." This means that touching a dead person after they are cold and before they are washed requires performing major ablution. Dead people emit diseases that cannot be removed except through major ablution.

The second way is what Shahīd Sayyid Muḥammad Bāqir al-Ṣadr ﷺ calls the social understanding of the text. An example is the narration of the Prophet ﷺ: "Whoever revives a dead plot of earth becomes its owner." If you go out and revive a plot through agriculture, you become its owner. The social understanding of this narration is that the effort that you put in entitles you to the plot. In the same way, if you write a book or create something, they are yours by right.

The third way is by abolishing specifications. An example is the narration from the Prophet ﷺ: "Do not compete except with three things: horses, she-camels, or arrows." Are other kinds of competing prohibited? Jurists have abolished this specification in favor of social benefits, such as athletic or charitable benefits.

The fourth way is induction. An example is the sound narration of ʿAbd al-Ṣamad b. Bashīr on the pilgrimage: "Any person who does something wrong without knowing is not culpable." If a person wears sewn (*makhīṭ*) clothes or walks in the shade (*taẓlīl*) during the pilgrimage out of unintentional ignorance is not culpable. The same thing applies to prayer. If a person used to recite the Fātiḥa and directly pray without reciting another *sūra* for years because they did not know, they don't have to make up those prayers. Due to the blessing of induction, we can generalize the ruling to include fasting. If a person inhales thick dust while fasting without knowing about the ruling, his fast remains valid. Another example is this. If a person crosses a long distance that constitutes traveling without the prior intention of staying in a place for ten days, they should shorten their prayers. There are only four places where a person has the choice between performing shortened and complete prayers; they are Mecca, Medina, al-Ḥā'ir of al-Ḥusayn عليه السلام, and the Grand Mosque of Kūfa. Some jurists like, Sayyid al-Murtaḍā قدس سره, extended this ruling to include the tombstones of all the Imāms عليهم السلام, while the author of *al-Jawāhir* [Shaykh Muḥammad Ḥasan al-Najafī] said that there is no text to support this ruling. Perhaps some jurists understood the reason behind the ruling [to include all the Imāms عليهم السلام], but most jurists say that the ruling particularly concerns al-Ḥā'ir of al-Ḥusayn عليه السلام.

5 Muḥarram, 1443 A.H.

The Symbol of the Perfect Human
Sayyidah al-Zahrāʾ ﷺ

"Should anyone argue with you concerning him, after the knowledge that has come to you, say, 'Come! Let us call our sons and your sons, our women and your women, our souls and your souls, then let us pray earnestly and call down God's curse upon the liars.'"[101]

The Features of the Perfect Human

Who is the Human Being?

"Certainly We created man from an extract of clay. Then We made him a drop of [seminal] fluid [lodged] in a secure abode. Then We created the drop of fluid as a clinging mass. Then We created the clinging mass as a fleshy tissue. Then We created the fleshy tissue as bones. Then We clothed the bones with flesh. Then We produced him as [yet] another creature. So blessed is God, the best of creators!"[102] We understand that this other creation is the human being. The tail of the verse "So blessed is God, the best of creators!"[103] implies that the creation of the human being is the very best creation; otherwise, why would God ﷻ be described as the best of creators? The reason for this status is that the essence of humanity includes four elements that other creatures do not have. They are reason, will, feeling, and

---

[101] Sūrat āl-ʿImrān, verse 61.

[102] Sūrat al-Muʾminūn, verses 12-14.

[103] Sūrat al-Muʾminūn, verse 14.

pure primordial nature (*fiṭra*). God ﷻ spoke of this pure primordial nature by saying, "So set your heart on the religion as a people of pure faith, the origination of God according to which He originated mankind. There is no altering God's creation."[104] He ﷻ explained it in the verse: "by the soul and Him who fashioned it, and inspired it with [discernment between] its virtues and vices."[105] This means that the human creature is distinct from other creatures because when it was fashioned, it was made to know virtues and vices.

What is the Purpose of the Human Being's Existence?

The purpose of the human's existence is attaining the status of representative (*vicegerency*) and being God's representative (*vicegerent*) on earth: "When your Lord said to the angels, 'Indeed I am going to set a viceroy on the earth,' they said, 'Will You set in it someone who will cause corruption in it, and shed blood, while we celebrate Your praise and proclaim Your sanctity?' He said, 'Indeed I know what you do not know.' And He taught Ādam the Names, all of them;1 then presented them to the angels and said, 'Tell me the names of these, if you are truthful.' They said, 'Immaculate are You! We have no knowledge except what You have taught us. Indeed You are the All-knowing, the All-wise.' He said,

[104] Sūrat al-Rūm, verse 30.

[105] Sūrat al-Shams, verses 7-8.

'O Ādam, inform them of their names.'"[106] Ādam 🌸
was a symbol of God's representative on earth, not in
himself but in his status as a human being. Every human
being became manifest in Ādam 🌸 in that moment as
an establisher of the position of representative:
"Certainly We created you, then We formed you, then
We said to the angels, 'Prostrate before Ādam.'"[107]
However, what does representative mean?

Sensory representation is the representation that is
based on the absence of the appointer and the presence
of the representative. But how can I be the
representative of God "and God is witness to all
things"[108]? The Qur'ān tells us, "And He is with you
wherever you may be,"[109] and in the supplication of
Imām ʿAlī 🌸, we read, "O God, you are the companion
in travel and the authority over family; only You can
bring them together." This is because God is witness to
all things.

The representative that we are talking about here is
actual representative, which means that the human
being is the mirror of God 🌸 in managing the affairs of
the universe: "Indeed We presented the Trust to the

---

[106] Sūrat al-Baqara, verses 30-33.

[107] Sūrat al-Aʿrāf, verse 11.

[108] Sūrat al-Burūj, verse 9.

[109] Sūrat al-Ḥadīd, verse 4.

heavens and the earth and the mountains, but they refused to bear it, and were apprehensive of it; but man undertook it. Indeed he is most unfair and senseless."[110] This trust is being the representative of God over the earth. Being God's representative in managing the universe necessitates building a civilization, but not a capitalist one fraught with wars and killing. It should be a civilization built on three pillars:

1. Justice: "Certainly We sent Our apostles with manifest proofs, and We sent down with them the Book and the Balance, so that mankind may maintain justice."[111]

2. Witnessing: "Thus We have made you a middle nation that you may be witnesses to the people, and that the Apostle may be a witness to you."[112]

3. Brotherhood: "The faithful are indeed brothers."[113]

How do we Achieve this Purpose?

1. Learning: No people can ever achieve progress unless they have knowledge. No people should take

---

[110] Sūrat al-Aḥzāb, verse 72.

[111] Sūrat al-Ḥadīd, verse 25.

[112] Sūrat al-Baqara, verse 143.

[113] Sūrat al-Ḥujurāt, verse 10.

pride in their past if their present is backwards. The only reason someone should feel a sense of pride in their actions is if their present is as good as their past. When a people exhibit knowledge, excellence, and uniqueness, they are entitled to pride: "And We draw these parables for mankind; but no one grasps them except those who have knowledge."[114]

2. The union of practical and theoretical reason: theoretical reason is the power of analysis and deduction whereas practical reason is the power of behavior that the Qur'ān calls the self-blaming soul: "And I swear by the self-blaming soul!;"[115] "by the soul and Him who fashioned it, and inspired it with [discernment between] its virtues and vices."[116]

3. There is a barrier between these two powers; sometimes a person does things they believe in and sometimes they do things that they don't believe in. They may also believe in things and not do them, whether out of fear, desire, or other reasons. In Sha'bān, we supplicate God ﷻ to remove this barrier: "O God, grant me perfect absorption in You, and light up the sights of our hearts with the light of looking at You, until the sights of the hearts

[114] Sūrat al-'Ankabūt, verse 43.

[115] Sūrat al-Qiyāma, verse 2.

[116] Sūrat al-Shams, verses 7-8.

> penetrate the veils of light and reach the mine of greatness, and our souls become attached to the glory of Your holiness." What does it mean for the sight to penetrate the veils of light? It requires the union of the practical and theoretical reason. How do we penetrate the veil between the two powers? If the veil is lifted, a person lives in tranquility, whereas if the veil remains, a person lives in worry. As long as worry is there, the veil is there: "Indeed man has been created covetous: anxious when an ill befalls him and grudging when good comes his way."[117] Tranquility comes with the removal of the veil. The way to do this is using the knowledge of the intellect to achieve the piety of the heart.

The Qur'ān features the concepts of knowledge (*al-ʿilm*) and the intellect (*al-ʿaql*) but not in the way we understand them. Knowledge in the Qur'ān is: "Is he who supplicates in the watches of the night, prostrating and standing, apprehensive of the Hereafter and expecting the mercy of his Lord . . . ? Say, 'Are those who know equal to those who do not know?' Only those who possess intellect take admonition."[118] Knowledge is tied to supplicating in the night; those who supplicate are considered those who know.

---

[117] Sūrat al-Maʿārij, verse 19.

[118] Sūrat al-Zumar, verse 9.

Turning scholarly materials to spiritual materials constitutes knowledge according to the Qurʾān. You are the same as a computer if you do not turn your information into knowledge of the heart: "God bears witness that there is no god except Him —and [so do] the angels and those who possess knowledge— maintainer of justice, there is no god but Him, the Almighty, the All-wise;"[119] "Only those of God's servants having knowledge fear Him."[120] The intellect in the Qurʾān means contemplating the universe and existence, reading them as a means to an end, and not a material reading like a physicist who is busy solving equations. We should read existence as a manifestation of God: "Soon We shall show them Our signs in the horizons and in their own souls until it becomes clear to them that He is the Real. Is it not sufficient that your Lord is witness to all things?"[121] "And who will [ever] renounce Ibrāhīm's creed except one who fools himself?"[122]

Prophet Ibrāhīm's ﷺ creed was outlined in the verses: "When night darkened over him, he saw a star and said, 'This is my Lord!' But when it set, he said, 'I do not like those who set.' Then, when he saw the moon rising, he

---

[119] Sūrat āl-ʿImrān, verse 18.

[120] Sūrat Fāṭir, verse 28.

[121] Sūrat al-Shūrā, verse 53.

[122] Sūrat al-Baqara, verse 130.

said, 'This is my Lord!' But when it set, he said, 'Had my Lord not guided me, I would surely have been among the astray lot.' Then, when he saw the sun rising, he said, 'This is my Lord! This is bigger!' But when it set, he said, 'O my people, indeed I disown what you take as [His] partners.' Indeed I have turned my face toward Him who originated the heavens and the earth, as a *ḥanīf*, and I am not one of the polytheists;'"[123] "And they will say, 'Had we listened or applied reason, we would not have been among inmates of the Blaze;'"[124] "Have they not traveled over the land so that they may have hearts by which they may apply reason."[125] If a person uses this knowledge [correctly], they will attain a sound heart: "Do not disgrace me on the day that they will be resurrected, the day when neither wealth nor children will avail, except him who comes to God with a sound heart."[126] Intellect is tied to ability and intellect and ability are both tied to wisdom.

---

[123] Sūrat al-An'ām, verses 76-78.

[124] Sūrat al-Mulk, verse 10.

[125] Sūrat al-Ḥajj, verse 46.

[126] Sūrat al-Shu'arā', verses 87-89.

What Are the Manifestations of God’s Representatives on the Earth?

Reaching the highest status of humanity: it is the status of Ādam and the status of learning and teaching. This is an elevated human characteristic. The angels objected. How is this being distinguished from the angels? “When your Lord said to the angels, ‘Indeed, I will set upon the earth a successive authority.’" The angels said, ‘Will You set upon it someone who will cause corruption in it, and shed blood, while we celebrate Your praise and sanctify you?’ He said, ‘Indeed I know what you do not know.’ And He taught Ādam the Names, all of them; then presented them to the angels and said, ‘Tell me the names of these, if you are truthful.’ They said, ‘Immaculate are You! We have no knowledge except what You have taught us. Indeed You are the All-knowing, the All-wise.’ He said, ‘O Ādam, inform them of their names,’ and when he had informed them of their names, He said, ‘Did I not tell you that I indeed know the Unseen in the heavens and the earth, and that I know whatever you disclose and whatever you were concealing?’”[127]

Uniqueness: Be unique in your character as a doctor, scholar, or professional; don’t be a copy of anyone else. It’s not important just to reach a certain position but to be unique in your position: “He, who created death and

[127] Sūrat al-Baqara, verses 30-33.

life, that He may test you [to see] which of you is best in conduct."[128] It has been narrated from Imām al-Kāẓim ﷺ that "a person who witnesses two equal days has lost." Living a lethal routine without distinction or development is a life of loss: "and say, 'My Lord! Increase me in knowledge.'"[129] This verse means that a person must keep on learning and not be content with a job or a position or a certain academic degree.

Support from the world of the unseen: "It is not [possible] for any human that God should speak to him except through revelation or from behind a curtain, or send a messenger who reveals by His permission whatever He wishes. Indeed He is all-exalted, all-wise."[130] May God speak to a person who is not a prophet? The answer is yes: "And when the angels said, 'O Maryam, God has chosen you and purified you, and He has chosen you above the world's women. O Maryam, be obedient to your Lord, and prostrate and bow down with those who bow [in worship].' These accounts are from the Unseen, which We reveal to you, and you were not with them when they were casting lots [to see] which of them would take charge of Maryam's care, nor were you with them when they were contending. When the angels said, 'O Maryam, God

---

[128] Sūrat al-Mulk, verse 2.

[129] Sūrat Ṭāhā, verse 114.

[130] Sūrat al-Shūrā, verse 51.

gives you the good news of a Word from Him whose name is Messiah, ʿĪsā, son of Maryam, distinguished in the world and the Hereafter, and one of those brought near [to God]."[131] Sayyidah Maryam ﷺ was spoken to; only prophets and apostles receive legislative revelation, but informative revelation includes anyone who is spiritually elevated. Prophet Ibrāhīm's wife, Sāra, was also spoken to: "His wife, standing by, laughed as We gave her the good news of [the birth of] Isḥāq, and of Yaʿqūb, after Isḥāq. She said, 'Oh, my! Shall I, an old woman, bear [children], and [while] this husband of mine is an old man?! That is indeed an odd thing!' They said, 'Are you amazed at God's dispensation? [That is] God's mercy and His blessings upon you, members of the household. Indeed He is all-laudable, all-glorious.'"[132]

Myths, Spiritual Stations, and Miracles from the World of the Unseen

Among the stations of Sayyidah al-Zahrāʾ ﷺ is that she was spoken to by the angels (*muḥaddatha*): "Peace upon you, O one knowledgeable and spoken to."[133] Shaykh al-Ṣadūq stated that the angels spoke to

---

[131] Sūrat āl-ʿImrān, verses 42-45.

[132] Sūrat Hūd, verses 71-73.

[133] [Translator's note]: The segment is from the visitation of Sayyidah al-Zahrāʾ ﷺ at the grave of the Prophet ﷺ.

Sayyidah al-Zahrā' 🌸 like they spoke to Maryam 🌸. Someone might say that these are only myths and legends, but this is untrue for several reasons:

The first reason is that the features of the perfect human have been discussed in the previous section. The Noble Qur'ān guaranteed that the perfect human will be spoken to like Maryam and Sāra were spoken to. If a perfect human applies the monotheism of theoretical and practical reason, they become prepared to be spoken to by the angels.

The second reason is that we are not talking to a person who does not believe in God 🕌 here. A person who believes in God 🕌 believes in the realms of creation and command, i.e. the worlds of witnessing and the unseen. The realm of creation is the world we are living in. This apparent material world is the world of sovereignty (*mulk*) that is surrounded by the world of dominion (*malakūt*). This is the first point. The second point is that the world of command and the world of the unseen dominate the world of witnessing and the world of creation. A material person only believes in this world, but if a person believes in both worlds, they will believe in the occurrences of both worlds. An example is the formation of human beings: "Then We created the drop of fluid as a clinging mass. Then We created the clinging mass as a fleshy tissue. Then We created the fleshy tissue as bones. Then We clothed the bones with flesh. Then We produced him as [yet] another creature. So blessed is

God, the best of creators!"[134] How did that unhearing and unseeing seminal matter turn into an intellect, a will, and emotions in twelve weeks? If the world of command did not interfere in the world of creation, it wouldn't have happened.

Someone may ask for a non-natural example of the interference of the world of the unseen in the world of witnessing, unlike the previous example that is natural. God ﷻ says, "Thereupon her Lord accepted her with gracious acceptance, and made her grow up in a worthy fashion, and He charged Zechariah with her care. Whenever Zechariah visited her in the sanctuary, he would find provisions with her. He said, 'O Mary, from where does this come for you?' She said, 'It comes from God. God provides whomever He wishes without any reckoning;'"[135] "and [he will be] a Prophet to the Children of Israel, [and he will declare,] 'I have certainly brought you a sign from your Lord: I will create for you out of clay the form of a bird, then I will breathe into it, and it will become a bird by God's leave. And I heal the blind and the leper and I revive the dead by God's leave."[136] How can all of this happen without interference? There is a point that people who don't believe in miracles raise. They say that these stories were

---

[134] Sūrat al-Mu'minūn, verse 14.

[135] Sūrat āl-'Imrān, verse 37.

[136] Sūrat āl-'Imrān, verse 49.

included in the Qur'ān as part of the time's culture, and that the Qur'ān itself does not approve of these miracles. The Arabs already knew these stories from the Torah and Evangel, and they were included in the Qur'ān simply on that basis.

The answer is that differentiating between the proofs of the verses does not make sense. In the verse: "Certainly God helped you at Badr, when you were abased [in the enemy's eyes]."[137] There is no doubt that the Battle of Badr actually happened. There is no doubt about the conquest of Mecca: "Alif, Lām, Mīm. Byzantium has been vanquished in a nearby territory, but following their defeat they will be victors."[138] Those people say that all the previous reports are true and actually happened, so why are the reports about the interference of the unseen in the case of Maryam based on the beliefs of the time? There is no logical explanation for judging some phenomena and not others and ignoring all those reports. What do those people say about the birth of Prophet 'Īsā ﷺ? Isn't it a religious truth? "Indeed the case of Jesus with God is like the case of Ādam: He created him from dust, then said to him, 'Be,' and he was."[139]

---

137 Sūrat āl-'Imrān, verse 123.

138 Sūrat al-Rūm, verses 1-3.

139 Sūrat āl-'Imrān, verse 59.

Let's assume we got past the issue of Prophet ʿĪsā 🕮. What can be said about: "Immaculate is He who carried His servant on a journey by night from the Sacred Mosque to the Farthest Mosque [al-Masjid al-Aqṣā] whose environs We have blessed, that We might show him some of Our signs"[140]? This is a report that the Prophet Muḥammad 🕮 was carried on a journey in one night. Isn't this a miracle from the world of the unseen? People who limit things to the material realm point out that the Farthest Mosque did not exist during the time of the Prophet Muḥammad 🕮; it was built by ʿAbd al-Malik b. Marwān after he had a disagreement with ʿAbdullāh b. al-Zubayr and couldn't enter Mecca. ʿAbd al-Malik b. Marwān built a dome on the rock and made it a mosque. Pay attention to the fallacy in this argument: the Farthest Mosque is not the same as the Dome of the Rock. A mosque is a place of worship; the Farthest Mosque is Jerusalem, but it is not that mosque with the copper dome [the Dome of the Rock]. Jerusalem contains the graves of Maryam, Isḥāq, and many prophets. The Farthest Mosque is not a building with the name "mosque" engraved on it; the Farthest Mosque is a place of worship. The Qurʾān says, "O Mary, be obedient to your Lord, and prostrate and bow down with those who bow [in worship]."[141] It is the place where Maryam 🕮 and the prophets 🕮

---

[140] Sūrat al-Isrāʾ, verse 1.

[141] Sūrat āl-ʿImrān, verse 43.

worshiped. The verse "Immaculate is He who carried His servant on a journey by night from the Sacred Mosque to the Farthest Mosque whose environs We have blessed, that We might show him some of Our signs"[142] involves interference from the world of the unseen.

When humans and God ﷻ speak, it is not a break in custom (*khāriq lil-'āda*); it is a conversation between the worlds of command and creation. God ﷻ also speaks to people through true visions. The true visions that many people see and predict events before they occur is simply a conversation between the worlds of command and creation. In that same way, God spoke to Sayyidah Maryam and Sayyidah al-Zahrā' ؑ.

Perfection in Sayyidah al-Zahrā's ؑ Character

The first feature: Sayyidah al-Zahrā' ؑ is a source of giving. She ؑ gave of her knowledge in the Fadak Sermon, and the *ḥadīths* that we have are enough to show the transcendence of Sayyidah al-Zahrā' ؑ. In addition, she is one of the five figures (*al-ashbāḥ al-khamsa*): "Indeed God desires to repel all impurity from you, O People of the Household, and purify you with a thorough purification."[143] The verse "Indeed the

[142] Sūrat al-Isrā', verse 1.

[143] Sūrat al-Aḥzāb, verse 33.

pious will drink from a cup seasoned with Kāfūr"[144] involves stations (*maqāmāt*) specific to Sayyidah al-Zahrā' ﷺ, and she is a manifestations of the Best Names (*al-asmā' al-ḥusnā*). It was also reported that the Prophet ﷺ said, "Fāṭimah is a piece of me; whoever angers her angers me" (*Ṣaḥīḥ al-Bukhārī*). The pleasure of God is linked to her ﷺ pleasure; this wouldn't have been the case if she wasn't a Proof of God. This is an expression of her infallibility and her attainment of the station of manifesting the Best Names. This means that Sayyidah al-Zahrā' ﷺ is a manifestation of God's knowledge, wisdom, and power. The narration from Abī 'Abd Allāh ﷺ regarding the verse "To God belong the Best Names, so supplicate Him by them"[145] states: "By God, we are the Best Names."

The second feature: Sayyidah al-Zahrā' ﷺ encompasses the Mother of the Book (*umm al-kitāb*). Of her special features, as you know, is the Book of Fāṭimah (*Muṣḥaf Fāṭima*). The Noble Qur'ān has two types of existences: material and unseen. The unseen Qur'ān is referred to as the Mother of the Book or the Hidden Book (*al-kitāb al-maknūn*). Whoever can reach the Qur'ān that's within the Preserved Tablet (*al-lawḥ al-maḥfūẓ*) or the Mother of the Book will know the meaning of the Qur'ān. Anyone who reaches that station understands

---

144 Sūrat al-Insān, verse 5.

145 Sūrat al-A'rāf, verse 180.

the verse: "We have sent down the Book to you as a clarification of all things"[146] and becomes able to understand the symbols and codes in the Qur'ān.

The Qur'ān itself tells us the identity of the people who can reach this station: "This is indeed a Noble Qur'ān, in a guarded Book, —no one reaches [*yamassuhu*] it except the pure ones."[147] The verb *massa* in Arabic does not mean touching but reaching: "Indeed God desires to repel all impurity from you, O People of the Household, and purify you with a thorough purification."[148] The Qur'ān explains itself by itself. Only God ﷻ and those grounded in knowledge know its interpretation. It has been said that the Book of Fāṭimah is not a Qur'ān but an interpretation of the Qur'ān.

The third feature: the third feature is supremacy: "And when the angels said, 'O Mary, God has chosen you and purified you, and He has chosen you above the world's women."[149] The exegetes say that the choosing mentioned in the verse refers to individualistic and not chronological comprehensiveness. The proof is the

---

[146] Sūrat al-Naḥl, verse 89.

[147] Sūrat al-Wāqi'a, verses 77-79 (translation modified slightly).

[148] Sūrat al-Aḥzāb, verse 33.

[149] Sūrat āl-'Imrān, verse 42.

verse: "Children of Israel, remember My blessing which I bestowed upon you, and that I gave you an advantage over all the nations."[150] However, the *umma* of the Prophet 🌸 is better: "You are the best nation [ever] brought forth for mankind: you bid what is right and forbid what is wrong."[151] This means that Sayyidah Maryam 🌸 is the best among the women of her time, but what about the period after her time? Sayyidah Maryam 🌸 is the mistress of the women of her world, and she was chosen over the women of the worlds, but Sayyidah Fāṭimah 🌸 became the mistress of the women of the worlds because she combined all merits and perfections.

The fourth feature: Sayyidah Fāṭimah 🌸 is the partner of the Prophet 🌸 in his message and mission. There is something called heavenly care (*al-ʿināya al-malakūtiyya*). We notice this in the verses related to Prophet Mūsā 🌸: "He said, 'Moses, your request has been granted! Certainly, We have done you a favor another time, when We revealed to your mother whatever was revealed: "Put him in the casket, and cast it into the river. Then the river will cast it on the bank, and he shall be picked up by an enemy of Mine and an enemy of his." And I cast upon you a love from Me, and that you might be reared under My eyes. When your

---

150 Sūrat al-Baqara, verse 47.

151 Sūrat āl-ʿImrān, verse 110.

sister walked up [to Pharaoh's palace] saying, "Shall I show you someone who will take care of him?" Then We restored you to your mother, so that she might be comforted and not grieve. Then you slew a soul, whereupon We delivered you from anguish, and We tried you with various ordeals. Then you stayed for several years among the people of Midian. Then you turned up as ordained, O Moses! And I chose you for Myself."[152]

Similarly, God ﷻ said about Maryam ﷺ: "When the wife of ʿImrān said, 'My Lord, I dedicate to You what is in my belly, in consecration. Accept it from me; indeed You are the All-hearing, the All-knowing.' And when she bore her, she said, 'My Lord, I have borne a female [child]' —and God knew better what she had borne— 'and the female is not like the male. I have named her Mary, and I commend her and her offspring to Your care against [the evil of] the outcast Satan.' Thereupon her Lord accepted her with gracious acceptance, and made her grow up in a worthy fashion, and He charged Zakariyyā with her care. Whenever Zechariah visited her in the sanctuary, he would find provisions with her. He said, 'O Mary, from where does this come for you?' She said, 'It comes from God. God provides whomever He wishes without any reckoning.'"[153] And Sayyidah

---

152 Sūrat Ṭā Hā, verses 36-41.

153 Sūrat āl-ʿImrān, verses 35-37.

Fāṭimah was like this too; she was born out of a tree in Paradise, she spoke to her mother and comforted her while still in the womb, and God gave the Prophet tidings of her: "Indeed We have given you *al-kawthar*."[154] *Al-Kawthar* is great abundance.

The Prophet Muḥammad said, "Fāṭimah is the mother of her father." Why did he say that? Sayyidah Fāṭimah used to lovingly inhale his scent, wipe the sweat off his brow, and hug him; she eased the burdens of prophethood and the mission for him. For this reason, he considered her his partner in the message. When the Christians of Najrān challenged him, he came out with her, her husband, and her two sons: "Should anyone argue with you concerning him, after the knowledge that has come to you, say, 'Come! Let us call our sons and your sons, our women and your women, our souls and your souls, then let us pray earnestly and call down God's curse upon the liars.'"[155] In order to challenge others in matters of religion, one must bring out people who are Proofs of God in His creation. The Prophet did not bring out any of his wives or companions on this occasion; he brought Imām ʿAlī.

[154] Sūrat al-Kawthar, verse 1 (translation modified slightly).

[155] Sūrat āl-ʿImrān, verse 61.

In the vows of mothers you remain

the essence of good fortune and blessings

We still lovingly guard

your eternal name upon our lips

Whenever "O Fāṭima" is called out

they hasten to say *ṣalawāt*, our spirits

Daughter of revelation and mother of guidance

you are young girls' revelation and mothers' guidance

Your great home made me stop

in the alleyway of memories

It was no ordinary home;

it was a capital of miracles

Tell us of your nights there

We care not for the talk of narrators

Were you with your right hand

the millstone turning?

Or was it life itself

that you were directing?

Did you spin yarn at your spindle

or were you spinning love among creation?

6 Muḥarram, 1443 A.H.

The Successful Figure and the Family

"O you who have faith! Save yourselves and your families from a Fire whose fuel is people and stones, over which are [assigned] angels, severe and mighty, who do not disobey whatever God has commanded them, and carry out what they are commanded."[156]

The Family from the Sociological Perspective

If the man and woman came to an agreement and the woman assumed the role of the mother while the man assumed the role of the father, is this a natural difference? The religious point of view is that this is a result of a difference in natural capacities and not social custom. There are two proofs of this:

1. Social pairings are a reflection of natural pairings: "In all things We have created pairs so that you may take admonition."[157] You are a pair in all things, just as you are a pair in human creation: "And of His signs is that He created for you mates from your own selves that you may take comfort in them, and He ordained affection and mercy between you. There are indeed signs in that for a people who reflect."[158] A man and a woman's feeling that they

---

[156] Sūrat al-Taḥrīm, verse 6.

[157] Sūrat al-Dhāriyāt, verse 49.

[158] Sūrat al-Rūm, verse 21.

are a pair naturally leads them to establish a family; they establish a family to fulfill their inclinations safely. In addition, females are naturally capable of motherhood and males are naturally capable of fatherhood.

2. The second proof is that if you review history, you will not find a time without the family unit. This is proof that the human race realized, from the first day, that safe procreation happens within the family. I emphasize the issue of safety here; I'm not talking about illegitimate means.

In contrast, the historical theory states that the family is a contract-based institution that was established over time; it is not a natural institution like the religious view states. We can offer the following critique of this view:

What do we mean by the word "natural"? Human society is not like a bee colony where the males and females have certain roles imposed on them. In the case of human beings, this is not a mandatory process; a person may die without having started a family. However, it is a natural process with the meaning that once the man and the woman do get together, they will naturally assume their proper roles. A man has the capacity of providing money and safety for the family, and the woman has the capacity of motherhood. Sociology is a critical science; it has criticized everything except the family because it considered the family a safe means of human procreation.

Is the Man the Leader?

There are three views in answer to this question.

1. The religious view: "Men are the managers of women, because of the advantage God has granted some of them over others, and by virtue of their spending out of their wealth."[159] The verse contains a precise expression that deserves attention. God said that men were the managers (*qawwāmūn*) and not the guardians (*awliyāʾ*) of women, although the word "guardian" was used elsewhere: "But if the debtor be feeble-minded, or weak, or incapable of dictating himself, then let his guardian dictate with honesty."[160] The word guardian implies absolute authority while the word manager implies responsibility. The man is responsible for ensuring the family's best interests; his role does involve some authority. In the visitation of Ahl al-Bayt 📿, we say, "Peace be upon you, O managers of creation with justice." In addition, God did not say that the man is better than the woman; He said, "Because of the advantage God has granted some of them over

---

[159] Sūrat al-Nisāʾ, verse 34.

[160] Sūrat al-Baqara, verse 282.

others."[161] A qualified man is better in this role, and the woman is better as a mother because she is qualified for this role.

2. The democratic view: The roles are based on discussion and agreement; neither the man nor the woman are leaders. Such a family will fail. The law states that leadership is a must or else society will fail. There must be a decisive leadership that has the final say.

3. The contractual view: After the pair contractually agree to marry, they agree about the identity of the leader. Actually, religion does not forbid this. It only states that if left to temperaments, the role of the manager will be the man's and not the woman's. Otherwise, the couple can choose whether to have children or not and how to distribute finances.

The Family's Positive Role

The family has several functions:

1. The family forms the identity of its members. It is a person's primary psychological center. Psychology says that a person has a need for belonging, and the family is the unit that fulfills this need. A person's sense of belonging is formed in the family. Edgar

[161] Sūrat al-Nisā', verse 34.

Morgan says that the family fulfills a person's need to belong.

2. A person's character is formed in the family. The family is the primary teacher of customs, knowledge, and traditions. The safety of society lies in the safety of the family; as long as the family is sound, society is sound.

3. Reinforcing cooperation: The family makes each member have patience when dealing with other people. This reinforces the acquisition of mutual skills, which is an expression of cooperation in society: "Cooperate in piety and Godwariness, but do not cooperate in sin and aggression."[162]

4. Getting a dose of reassurance: Each person has worries and needs a dose of reassurance. If the family is close, it is the best source for getting reassurance: "And of His signs is that He created for you mates from your own selves that you may take comfort in them, and He ordained affection and mercy between you."[163]

---

[162] Sūrat al-Mā'ida, verse 2.

[163] Sūrat al-Rūm, verse 21.

The Characteristics of a Successful Person

How to Become Successful?

Having a character means having a number of values. Boltog has a book on how children can succeed. In it, he says that the psychologist Martin Seligman cooperated with the famous psychologist Christopher Peterson and they coauthored a statistical and diagnostic book of psychological disorders. In their book, the authors said that there are twenty-four character traits that are either active, such as courage, wisdom, and integrity, or passive such as when admire and appreciate the efforts of others. There are also character traits that are based on social intelligence. Social intelligence means the ability to communicate and adapt with other people. I should point out that when I mention the opinions of Western scholars, it doesn't mean that I believe that they are set in stone. The matter is simply that these opinions are scholarly and based on deductions, and they simulate reality: "who listen to the word and follow the best [sense] of it."[164]

The Building Blocks of Character

Family stability: Philippa Perry wrote a book called *The Book You Wish Your Parents Had Read*. In it, she says that the important thing is not to establish a family but

---

[164] Sūrat al-Zumar, verse 18.

to have a calm family environment. There must be respect between the man and the woman even if they are separated. This is because if the family environment is unstable, the child will feel guilty because she has a bond with both parents. In reality, however, there is no household where the father and mother do not disagree. How should we manage disagreements within the family? We should not ignore disagreements because ignoring them would just widen the gap and extinguish the emotions. You do not manage disagreements by keeping score as though it is a match. The goal is to address the disagreement and not to win points.

Consideration of feelings: While having a disagreement, feelings must be considered. The word "you" is a word of aggression that stings and worsens disagreements. Say, "I'm unhappy with how things happened." Don't use you-statements.

Establishing affection: Affection needs to be nurtured. In 1986, John Gottman established a lab in Washington called the Love Lab. Gottman mentioned ways to establish affection between friends and couples:

1. Responding to communication: Join me in reading a book or go to lunch or dinner with me.

2. Offering praise: stop criticizing and blaming because that puts an end to affection. Use positive reinforcement.

3. Respecting the other opinion: You, the man, are not infallible and she is not infallible. Leave space for accepting one another's others' opinion. 'Alī and Sayyidah Fāṭimah 🌸 are the best example of harmony. It has been narrated that Sayyidah Fāṭimah 🌸 asked Imām 'Alī 🌸, "O cousin, did you know me as a traitor or a liar ever since we came into each other's company?" He 🌸 said, "God forbid! You are more righteous and pious than to even be scolded." As for Imām 'Alī's 🌸, he said, "By God, I never angered her or forced her to do anything until God took her away. As for her, she never angered me or disobeyed me. I used to look at her and forget my worries and sadness."

Positivity: A positive person always accepts simple explanations whereas a negative person complicates things. When a negative person fails an exam, they say, "I'm stupid," which implies that they will stay like that. If they say instead, "I didn't prepare enough," things would change. Another example is that if a negative person breaks up with his fiancée, he says, "No one loves me." The Prophet 🌸 said, "Hope for good and you will find it." When a man called Suhayl b. 'Āmir arrived, the Prophet 🌸 said, "Things just got easy (sahl) for you because Suhayl came." This means that even the mention of a name with a positive meaning made the Prophet 🌸 optimistic. Positivity is a skill that should be acquired, but this shouldn't be done excessively. Imām

ʿAlī ﷺ says, "A reasonable person relies on his efforts and an ignorant person relies on his hopes."

Willpower and self-control: The standard of heroism is self-control and not lineage, fortune, or physique. A hero is not someone who walks a long road but someone who fears God. Some people are addicted to smoking; you tell them that it's harmful and they say that they know but can't quit. A man came to Imām al-Ṣādiq ﷺ and said, "I am addicted to eating dirt." The Imām ﷺ told him, "All it requires is a bit of manly resolve."

How can we nurture willpower in our children? A narration states that you should give the child certain responsibilities. The Prophet ﷺ says, "Do not exhaust your child or call him names." This means that parents should give children some chores so that they will learn to rely on themselves: let them prepare their own food or make their beds. Not calling a child names means that you shouldn't hurtfully point out their faults, shame them, or remind them of their mistakes. Parents should treat their children between these two boundaries: "Forbearance (*ḥilm*) and patience are a result of a greatness of spirit (*ʿuluww al-himma*)."

Motivation: All values require the two elements of initiative and perseverance. For example, you tell your child to learn how to pray. That needs initiative and perseverance. The presence of these two elements in the first place requires incentives. Tell your child about the benefits of prayer to make him practice maintaining his prayers. It has been narrated that the Prophet ﷺ heard a Bedouin praying and approved of his prayer. The Prophet ﷺ asked the man, "What clan do you belong to?" He said, "The clan of ʿĀmir b. Ṣaʿṣaʿa." The Prophet ﷺ asked, "Do you know why I approved of your prayer?" The man said, "It's because we are related." The Prophet ﷺ replied, "Relations have due rights, but I approved of your prayer because you supplicated your Lord well."

Conscientiousness: Psychology contains a branch called the science of the character, which tells you how to study personality traits. There are five personality traits: neuroticism, agreeableness, openness, extraversion, and conscientiousness. Conscientiousness means having a sense of responsibility, expressed in the Qurʾān as follows: "And I swear by the self-blaming soul!;"[165] "by the soul and Him who fashioned it, and inspired it with [discernment between] its virtues and vices."[166] This trait means that a child should excel in their studies, be organized, be a good spouse in the future, and not transgress anyone's rights. The noble textual evidence that we have focuses greatly on the conscience. The Prophet ﷺ says, "Hold your own selves accountable

[165] Sūrat al-Qiyāma, verse 2.

[166] Sūrat al-Shams, verses 7-8.

before you are held accountable and weigh yourselves before they are weighed for you." When Jundub wanted to praise Imām ʿAlī 🕮, he said, "By God, he wept greatly and contemplated deeply. He held himself accountable in private and wrung his hands about past events."

Avoiding luxuries: Suniya Luthar conducted a comparative study between children who come from low-income and high-income families respectively. I'm not saying all rich families are like this, but the study indicated that depression, drugs, and smoking are all more common in rich families. The cause of all of those things is a luxurious lifestyle. It is a luxury to overprotect a child. Teach your child what deprivation is. Imām al-Bāqir 🕮 says, "My father saw a father and son walking together, with the son leaning heavily on his father's arm. My father despised the man so much that he did not speak to him until he died."

Appreciating beauty: I mean moral beauty; the beauty of honesty, trustworthiness, and keeping our promises. We raise our children to appreciate the beauty of honesty and other values: "those who spend in ease and adversity, and suppress their anger, and excuse [the faults of] the people, and God loves the virtuous."[167] We should teach our children to taste the sweetness of prayer. If a child does not learn to pray from a young age, when will they learn? Prayer gives a sense of peace;

---

[167] Sūrat āl-ʿImrān, verse 134.

it is the offering that draws every pious person closer to God. It has been narrated from Imām al-Ṣādiq ﷺ that he said, "Tell your children to pray when they reach seven years old."

A person can acquire all the components of a successful family and character from the family of Sayyidah Fāṭimah and Imām 'Alī ﷺ: "Indeed God desires to repel all impurity from you, O People of the Household, and purify you with a thorough purification."[168] This is a family of martyrs who refused oppression and stood up to tyranny. This is a family that taught the *umma*.

7 Muḥarram, 1443 A.H.

[168] Sūrat al-Aḥzāb, verse 33.

The Best Example of Marital Life
Imām ʿAlī and Sayyidah Fāṭimah ﻋﻠﻴﻬﻤﺎ ﺍﻟﺴﻼﻡ

"And of His signs is that He created for you mates from your own selves that you may take comfort in them, and He ordained affection and mercy between you. There are indeed signs in that for a people who reflect."[169]

The Views on Marital Life

What Is Marital Life?

There are many movements, disciplines, and concepts on the topic. John Gray states that psychologists base marital life on two pillars: the equality between men and women and understanding one another as a basis for success. In such a case, the couple devotes the differences between them to establish harmony and connection. This is marital life according to psychology. What about sociology? Modern sociologists say that there is no way to avoid the fact that marital life has changed in the modern age due to the diversity of its forms. In the past, marital life had rules and rights, and was a burden to both spouses, but today there is more freedom. The couple themselves decide their roles and even decide if they want to separate.

As for the feminist movement, some of its supporters view marriage as a prison that confines the woman's capacities. Some radical branches went so far as to allow open relations and sexual instincts that are separate

---

[169] Sūrat al-Rūm, verse 21.

from motherhood. This has led to disasters in the West. 4% of men may raise a child who is not related to them. There is even a series that went on for nineteen seasons where the woman gathers all the men whom she had relations with for a DNA test. One woman had eighteen different men tested and none of them was a match with her son.

What Is Marital Life in Religious Thought?

The answer to this question is found in three verses: "And of His signs is that He created for you mates from your own selves that you may take comfort in them, and He ordained affection and mercy between you. There are indeed signs in that for a people who reflect."[170] The language of the verse is beautiful and inspiring. "Of His signs"[171]: this means that marriage is one of God's signs. "He created for you [*lakum*]..."[172] Why? Marriage is a manifestation of humankind's primordial nature and their inclination to love, mercy, tranquility, and peace. All these inclinations become manifest and are organized through marriage. The exegesis of this part of the verse in *Tafsīr al-Rāzī* is that it means "He created for your benefit," i.e. He created the woman to serve the man. However, this is not correct. The letter *lām* in the

---

[170] Sūrat al-Rūm, verse 21.

[171] Sūrat al-Rūm, verse 21.

[172] Sūrat al-Rūm, verse 21.

word *lakum* indicates specification (*lām al-ikhtiṣāṣ*). An example is when we say, "This sum of money is for this car (*hadhā al-mablagh li-hadhihi al-sayyāra*)." This means that there is between men and women a primordial connection, which is marital life. This was followed by the phrase "that you may take comfort."[173]

The second verse is "they are a garment for you, and you are a garment for them."[174] The need for this garment is to cover up faults, adorn oneself, fend off hot weather, and get warm. The woman is the man's adornment and the man is the woman's adornment. A woman covers up the man's faults and each of them is the other's warm shelter.

The third verse is "Consort with them in an honorable manner."[175]

Marital Life in Religious Thought

The man needs flowing emotion. A man came to the Prophet ﷺ and said, "I have a woman who comes to meet me when I enter and walks me out when I leave. Whenever she sees me burdened with worries, she says, 'Don't worry. If you are worried about your sustenance,

---

173 Sūrat al-Rūm, verse 21.

174 Sūrat al-Baqara, verse 187.

175 Sūrat al-Nisāʾ, verse 19.

there is One ensuring it for you, but if you are worried about your Hereafter, may God increase your worry." The Prophet ﷺ told the man, "Give her tidings of Paradise and tell her, 'You are one of God's workers, and every day you get the reward of seventy martyrs." The woman's love for the man ensures the continuation of the family. The Prophet ﷺ says, "When a man tells his wife, 'I love you,' it will never be erased from her heart."

There must be a calm sexual atmosphere. Sexual relations are not like surgery, and the woman is not the man's toy. The woman must stimulate the man by her beauty because this motivates chastity in both of them. Al-Ḥasan b. Jahm saw al-Kāẓim عليه السلام dyeing his hair. Imām al-Kāẓim عليه السلام said, "If you do not adorn yourself, would it please you to see her doing the same thing?" Al-Ḥasan b. Jahm said, "It would not." The Imām عليه السلام said, "There you go then." This means that the man should adorn himself for his wife and the woman should adorn herself for her husband. Both need to adorn themselves to produce a fruitful environment.

There must be a sharing of responsibilities; many men dump everything on the women. There must be a partnership in managing the affairs of the home. Look at Imām ʿAlī and Sayyidah Fāṭimah عليهما السلام: Imām ʿAlī عليه السلام took it upon himself to bring firewood and water and sweep the house, and Sayyidah Fāṭimah عليها السلام took it upon herself to grind the grain, knead the dough, and bake the bread. Imām ʿAlī and Sayyidah Fāṭimah عليهما السلام told the

Prophet ﷺ to divide their chores, so he ﷺ made Sayyidah Fāṭimah عليها السلام responsible for indoor chores and Imām ʿAlī عليه السلام responsible for outdoor chores.

There must be a feeling of mutual contentment. The Prophet ﷺ visited Imām ʿAlī and Sayyidah Fāṭimah عليهما السلام a day after their marriage. He ﷺ asked Imām ʿAlī عليه السلام, "How did you find your wife?" Imām ʿAlī عليه السلام said, "She is the best supporter in obeying God." When the Prophet ﷺ asked Sayyidah Fāṭimah عليها السلام the same question, she said, "He is praiseworthy husband."

The Happy Marriage

The happy marriage has several pillars:

1. Prior affection of the heart: Marry the woman your heart inclines to. Abū Yaʿfūr narrated from al-Ṣādiq عليه السلام the following. "I said that I wanted to marry a woman but my father wanted me to marry someone else. He عليه السلام said, 'Marry the one you love, not the one your parents love.'"

2. Detailed knowledge of the other person: The man should know the woman and the woman should know the man in detail and through lawful means. What are the man's conceptions of family life? How capable is he of understanding the woman's feelings and diffusing disagreements? The same questions also apply to the woman. The third characteristic is

religious knowledge, and the fourth is a religious reservation against relationships, showing off beauty in front of others (*tabarruj*), and so on. The Prophet ﷺ said, "If someone comes to ask for your daughter's hand in marriage and you approve of his morals and religion, accept his proposal. 'Unless you do it, there will be turmoil on the earth and great corruption.'"[176] The Prophet ﷺ also said, "The best of your women is fertile, amiable, chaste, and dignified." Imām al-Ṣādiq ؑ said, "The best of your women smells pleasant and cooks delicious food. When she spends, she spends judiciously and when she saves money, she saves money judiciously."

3. Love and appreciation: John Gray has a book called *Men Are from Mars, Women Are from Venus*. It is one of the most influential books over the last quarter of the twentieth century. Many people read it, and it helped a lot of families. Things changed over time, so he later wrote another book called *Beyond Mars and Venus*.

There Are Five Differences Between Men and Women

1. Men are usually indifferent. Women's moods change like a wave; this is because of hormonal changes.

---

[176] Sūrat al-Anfāl, verse 73 (translation changed slightly).

2. Men communicate with women for a purpose. Women consider communication itself a purpose.

3. Women want men to understand them before they even speak. This causes problems sometimes.

4. Men enjoy sexual relations with their wives, whereas women enjoy romance, suggestiveness, and displays of emotion.

5. Feelings should be shared rather than waiting for the other person to speak first and show appreciation.

John Gray also says that Abraham Maslow set out a hierarchy of needs, divided into primary and secondary needs. Women today focus on secondary needs. Forty years ago, women viewed men as providing safety and financial support, which are primary needs. Today, women await emotional fulfillment because they no longer need financial support, and men no longer view women only as housekeepers. There is a need for emotional fulfillment; both men and women need love and appreciation, but the ways of doing that are different.

A woman doesn't only want the man to bring in money. She wants someone who understands her feelings, listens to her, participates in her projects, and asks her about any challenges she may be facing. This is how women believe love and appreciation should be expressed.

A man waits for appreciation more than anything else. A woman's need for appreciation can be likened to dessert after a meal; for the man, appreciation is the main course. The woman should admire the man because that strengthens his self-confidence.

The Perfect Marriage: Imām ʿAlī and Sayyidah Fāṭimah ﷺ

When we observe societies experiencing sectarian strife, we thank God for our societies. There is nothing between the Sunna and the Shīʿa but brotherly understanding, cooperation, and complementarity. As Dr. Muḥammad al-ʿĪsā says, the Shīʿa consider the Sunna as their counterparts and the opposite is true. Both participate in building up the same homeland. Real, true citizenship means that all people participate in building their homelands, which we noticed before Dr. Muḥammad al-ʿĪsā even spoke. The spirit of sectarianism has decreased and the spirit of honest citizenship and harmony has become established. Jobs should be given based on competence regardless of whether the person is a Sunnī or a Shīʿī. Competence is the standard, without regard to tribal or ethnic affiliations. Notice how our great *marājiʿ* say that the Sunna are not our brothers but our own selves.

Imām ʿAlī and Sayyidah Fāṭima's عليهما السلام marriage has several features:

1. Humanitarianism: Each spouse should make the other feel like an equal. If someone thinks that their spouse is less than them, this may cause a problem.

2. Perfection: "Put on your adornment on every occasion of prayer;"[177] "To mankind has been made to seem decorous the love of [worldly] desires, including women and children, accumulated piles of gold and silver, horses of mark, livestock, and farms. Those are the wares of the life of this world."[178] What is the difference between these two kinds of adornment? There is a true kind of adornment and an external kind of adornment. External adornments are like beautiful clothes and luxury cars. As for true adornments, they're different. Marriage is considered an establishment of culture, and Imām ʿAlī and Sayyidah Fāṭimah عليهما السلام gave birth to giants. What did Sayyidah Fāṭima's عليها السلام furniture and dowry consist of? A rug from Hajar [in Bahrain], a cup for drinking milk, a waterskin, a wooden clothes hanger, soft sand for the inside of the home, and two mattresses. When Imām ʿAlī عليه السلام gave Sayyidah Fāṭimah عليها السلام these things, the

[177] Sūrat al-Aʿrāf, verse 31.

[178] Sūrat āl-ʿImrān, verse 14.

Prophet ﷺ said, "O God, bless people who have earthenware utensils."

3. Education: Imām ʿAlī and Sayyidah Fāṭimah عليهما السلام were an example for all generations.

4. Emotion: Sayyidah Fāṭimah عليها السلام asked Imām ʿAlī عليه السلام, "O cousin, did you know me as a traitor or a liar ever since we came into each other's company?" He عليه السلام said, "God forbid! You are more righteous and pious than to even be scolded." As for Imām ʿAlī's عليه السلام, he said, "By God, I never angered her or forced her to do anything until God took her away. As for her, she never angered me or disobeyed me. I used to look at her and forget my worries and sadness."

5. Spirituality: "Through the intellect God is worshipped." You should use the material world to focus on building up the spirit and its values. Imām ʿAlī عليه السلام told a man from the clan of Saʿd, "Would you like me to tell you about Fāṭimah and I? We lived together and she was the Prophet's most beloved family member. She filled the waterskin so often that it left a mark on her chest, and she turned the grindstone so often that the skin on her hand became thick, and she swept so often that her clothes became dusty, and she lit fires under the pot so often until her clothes became black. This caused her great harm. I asked her, 'Why don't you go to your father and ask him for a servant to spare you

the trouble of all this work?' She went to the Prophet, but she found people talking together in his house, so she felt shy and left. The Prophet found out that she came because she needed something, so he came to us while we were under our blanket. He said to us, 'Peace upon you, you two under the blanket.' We kept quiet because we were shy. He said again, 'Peace upon you.' We worried that if we did not respond, he would leave. He used to do that: he would greet people three times. If he was not asked to enter, he would leave. For this reason, I said, 'And peace be upon you, O Prophet of God. Come in.' As soon as he sat by our heads, he asked, 'What did you need from Muḥammad yesterday, O Fāṭima?' We worried that if we did not answer him, he would leave. I popped my head out of the blanket and said, 'By God, I will tell you, O Prophet of God. She filled the waterskin so often that it left a mark on her chest, and she turned the grindstone so often that the skin on her hands became thick, and she swept so often that her clothes became dusty, and she lit fires under the pot so often until her clothes became black. I asked her, 'Why don't you go to your father and ask him for a servant to spare you the trouble of all this work?' The Prophet told us, 'How about I teach you something that is better for you than a servant? If you lie down to sleep, say *subḥān Allāh* thirty-three times, *al-ḥamdulillāh* thirty-three times, and

Allāhu akbar thirty-four times.' At this, Sayyidah Fāṭimah popped her head out of the blanket and said, 'I am content with God and His Prophet. I am content with God and His Prophet. I am content with God and His Prophet.'"

8 Muḥarram, 1443 A.H.

The Exemplar in Giving
Sayyidah al-Zahrāʾ ﷺ

"We have enjoined man concerning his parents: His mother carried him through weakness upon weakness, and his weaning takes two years. Give thanks to Me and to your parents. To Me is the return."[179]

Motherhood may be discussed under three different headings.

Motherhood: A Human Necessity

The Definition of Motherhood

Linguistically, motherhood (*umūma*) relates to origins. The mother (*al-umm*) of something is its origin: "It is He who has sent down to you the Book. Parts of it are definitive verses, which are the mother of the Book [*umm al-kitāb*]."[180] This means that there is a group of definitive verses that are Qur'ānic rules and principles: "Alif, Lām Rā. [This is] a Book, whose signs have been made definitive and then elaborated, from One [who is] all-wise, all-aware."[181] In sociology, motherhood is a bond between two people; one of them is the origin: "their mothers are only those who bore them."[182] The

---

[179] Sūrat Luqmān, verse 14.

[180] Sūrat āl-ʿImrān, verse 7.

[181] Sūrat Hūd, verse 1.

[182] Sūrat al-Mujādila, verse 2.

mother is the one who produces the egg; giving birth is not necessary for motherhood. When the Qur'ān talks about motherhood, it focuses on the dual aspects of pain and security. Concerning pain, the Qur'ān says, "We have enjoined man concerning his parents: His mother carried him through weakness upon weakness;"[183] "His mother has carried him in travail [*kurhan*], and bore him in travail."[184] Travail means hardship, and not hatred (*karāha*).

Is motherhood a human necessity or is it a replaceable social role? Some feminist movements have ignored the role of motherhood. Simone de Beauvoir says in her book that the sanctity surrounding the role of motherhood is forced and that motherhood is the reason for women's setbacks. Radical feminism stated that motherhood was constraining the woman within the home, which led young women to refuse motherhood. According to CDC statistics in 2007, birth rates declined to 7%, later reaching 4% during the pandemic. What are the alternatives to motherhood?

1. Daycares: Women give birth and daycares assume the role of motherhood. It has been found that the presence of children in these daycares make them lose faith in their own families. This is because the

---

183 Sūrat Luqmān, verse 14.

184 Sūrat al-Aḥqāf, verse 15.

family in this case is no longer the place for education and transmitting values.

2. Renting: In this case, motherhood becomes an economic opportunity and a career. However, it was discovered that this (proposed) solution is also a failure because only the biological mother is able to lovingly and tenderly keep up with the child in all the stages of development. Some families now even leave the child to their maid.

3. Relying on the father: Despite this option, studies emphasize that the man does not have the required emotional energy that the child needs in the first two years.

Mary Wollstonecraft, one of the pioneers of feminism, says that women in these times became more capable of motherhood than they were a century ago. This is because they became educated and more cultured. Carol Gilligan says that relationships are of two types: balanced and unbalanced. Balanced relationships are relationships between two equals such as friends. Unbalanced relationships are between givers and receivers such as between teachers and students. Motherhood is the best example of an unbalanced relationship.

The Elements of Motherhood

1. The physiological element: all women have an inclination to be mothers. A little girl takes a doll and pretends that this doll is her child. All mammals undergo certain chemical changes. Estrogen is the hormone that prepares the mother for motherhood, as well as prolactin, which is considered the love hormone.

2. The personal element: A mother can tell how her child is feeling even if the child doesn't say a word. She knows her child best.

3. The sociological element: There are studies that compared children that go to daycare and children that stay with their families. These studies concluded that a child who experiences natural motherhood is healthier and more normal. When this child hears his mother's heartbeat, he feels secure. A mother's milk is the best kind of milk for the growth of the brain. Motherhood is a journey during which the mother constantly gives, but she benefits too. A child acquires language and a sense of self, and a mother learns new things as she educates her child.

4. The psychological element: educating the child strengthens the mother by giving her willpower and endurance. At the social level, she becomes gentler

and more flexible due to dealing with children and their moods.

5. The element of values: How often did we wrong our mothers? Thanks to the education our mothers gave us, we acquire the ability to forgive and excuse wrongs because our mothers themselves live by that spirit of forgiveness.

6. The administrative element: The mother is the central point of the family and everyone holds on to her. The journey of motherhood gives her administrative skills that may be applied cleverly and quickly.

All this proves that the role of motherhood is irreplaceable.

Divine Attention to Motherhood

"We have enjoined man concerning his parents: His mother carried him through weakness upon weakness."[185] The Qur'ān focuses on honoring one's parents (*birr al-wālidayn*): "We have enjoined man concerning his parents: His mother carried him through weakness upon weakness, and his weaning takes two years. Give thanks to Me and to your parents. To Me is

[185] Sūrat Luqmān, verse 14.

the return."[186] It is reported that the Prophet ﷺ said, "Paradise is under mothers' feet." A man came to the Prophet ﷺ and asked, "O Prophet of God, whom should I honor?" The Prophet ﷺ said, "Your mother." The man asked, "Then whom?" The Prophet ﷺ said, "Your mother." The man asked, "Then whom?" The Prophet ﷺ said, "Your mother." The man asked, "Then whom?" The Prophet ﷺ said, "Your father." It has also been reported that if you were offering additional voluntary prayers (*nāfila*) and your father calls for you, you should not interrupt your prayers, but that if your mother calls for you, you should answer her.

There is a book written by Daniel J. Siegel and Tina Payne Bryson called *The Whole-Brain Child.* The book states that all fathers and mothers worry about their children, so how can we relieve this worry? The way to do that is not through perfect education because that is rare. The mother doesn't even have to read educational books. It's enough to rely on two pillars:

1. Family presence and stability: This involves eating at the same table. This creates an atmosphere of stability and calm within the family. It also involves sharing, such as sharing the other person's worries, and empathy, which means that when a family member has a problem, everyone should care. Another requirement is presence, i.e. being

[186] Sūrat Luqmān, verse 14.

physically and emotionally present. It's no use if you are there but are staring at your phone the whole time. You must nurture the child and answer their questions.

2. Secure attachment: It is based on three things:

    a. Feeling protected.

    b. Feeling understood by having questions answered as soon as they are asked. If the father or mother do not give an answer, the child will look for the answer elsewhere.

    c. Feeling calm.

These three feelings cannot develop by leaving the child to the maid.

Attachment to the mother develops the positive mind that has many manifestations and effects:

1. Self-worth: "and as for your Lord's blessing, proclaim it!"[187] Self-worth is essential in personal development.

---

[187] Sūrat al-Ḍuḥā, verse 11.

2. Impulse regulation: “[those who] suppress their anger, and excuse [the faults of] the people, and God loves the virtuous.”[188]

3. Academic excellence: “who listen to the word [of God] and follow the best [sense] of it. They are the ones whom God has guided, and it is they who possess intellect.”[189]

4. Social intelligence: Look at your child. Can he adapt socially? Luqmān tells his son, “O my son! Maintain the prayer and bid what is right and forbid what is wrong, and be patient through whatever may visit you. That is indeed the steadiest of courses. Do not turn your cheek disdainfully from the people, and do not walk exultantly on the earth. Indeed God does not like any swaggering braggart.”[190]

5. Leadership: The Qur’ān says that people who have leadership qualities are more secure and calm: “The servants of the All-beneficent are those who walk humbly on the earth, and when the ignorant address them, say, ‘Peace!’”[191]

---

[188] Sūrat āl-‘Imrān, verse 134.

[189] Sūrat al-Zumar, verse 18.

[190] Sūrat Luqmān, verse 18-19.

[191] Sūrat al-Furqān, verse 63.

Generous Motherhood and Sayyidah al-Zahrāʾ عليها السلام

Generous motherhood has several features:

1. Emotional stability: The father was the Prophet Muḥammad ﷺ and the mother was Sayyidah Khadīja عليها السلام. The Prophet ﷺ always mentioned Sayyidah Khadīja عليها السلام; he never forgot her. One of his ﷺ other wives once told him, "What makes you mention a woman so old that she became toothless? God gave you a better replacement of her." The Prophet ﷺ responded, "God did not give me a better replacement. She believed in me when the people disbelieved in me, she believed in me when the people called me a liar, and she supported me with her money when the people withheld their money, and God gave me children from her and not from other women." Sayyidah Fāṭimah عليها السلام acquired emotional stability from her own family and gave it to her children. She عليها السلام danced with Imām al-Ḥasan and Imām al-Ḥusayn عليهما السلام and called them the apple of her eye and the fruit of her heart.

2. Practical application of values: Sayyidah al-Zahrāʾ عليها السلام gave others advice only in a few narrations because she عليها السلام was concerned with applying values practically. Imām al-Ḥasan عليه السلام said, "I did not see anyone who worshipped more than my mother Sayyidah Fāṭima, and I never saw her supplicating for her own sake."

3. Focusing on natural values: Cultural values are acquired and may be learned from society, but natural values can only come from the mother. A child is born with these values:

   a. The connection to God ﷻ: The first value is having a connection to God ﷻ and knowing that God ﷻ is the refuge. You enter the homes of some families and hear music being played while "the angels attend the home where the Qur'ān is read." Let the child hear you speak Godly words. This has two effects. The first is establishing a barrier against sins. It is reported that the Prophet ﷺ looked at some children and said, "Woe to the children of the last days from their parents." He ﷺ was asked, "O Prophet of God, do you mean that their polytheist parents?" He ﷺ said, "No, I mean their faithful parents. They will teach them nothing about religious obligations, and if the children try to learn on their own, they stop them and be content with a small piece of this world. I have nothing to do with them, and they have nothing to do with me." The second effect is that a child who is used to supplicating has a stronger will. Yūsuf (عليه السلام) was thrown in the well at nine years old but he (عليه السلام) was connected to God. Sayyidah Fāṭimah (عليها السلام) was like this too. On Laylat al-Qadr, she (عليها السلام) put her children to sleep during the day so that they could stay awake during the night, giving them less food so that they would not feel too full [to worship]. Sayyid Ibn Ṭāwūs narrated in his *Muhaj al-Da'awāt* that Salmān said the following: "Fāṭimah taught me some words that she had learned from the Prophet and that she repeated every day and night. She told me, 'If you'd like to never suffer the harm of a fever as long as you live, say this regularly: in the name of God. In the name of God, the light of all light. In the name of God, light upon light. In the name of God, the provider of all things. In the name of God who created light from light. Thanks be to God who created light from light and let the light shine on the mountain in the Book inscribed on an unrolled parchment, in an allotted lot, upon a blessed Prophet. Thanks be to God who is mentioned for His might, known for His pride, and thanked in good and bad times. May God send His blessings on Muḥammad and his pure family."

b. Understanding life objectively: Our lives are like God's ﷻ saying, "Certainly We have created for hell many of the jinn and humans: they have hearts with which they do not understand, they have eyes with which they do not see, they have ears with which they do not hear. They are like cattle; rather they are more astray. It is they who are the heedless."[192] Life is a lesson, not a permanent stay: "By the means of what God has given you, seek the abode of the Hereafter, while not forgetting your share of this world."[193] The Prophet ﷺ saw Sayyidah Fāṭimah ؑ covered with a camel hair-blanket while turning the millstone and breastfeeding her baby. The Prophet ﷺ became tearful and said, "O daughter, I give you tidings that the bitterness of this world will be swept away by the sweetness of the Hereafter." Sayyidah Fāṭimah ؑ said, "O Prophet of God, praise be to God for His blessings, and thanks be to God for His bounties."

c. Unlimited giving: This was the case since the Day of the Vow: "They fulfill their vows and fear a day whose ill will be widespread. They give food, for the love of Him, to the needy, the orphan and the prisoner, [saying,] 'We feed you only for the sake of God. We do not want any reward from you nor any thanks."[194] Imām al-Ḥasan ؑ was five, Imām al-Ḥusayn ؑ was four, and Sayyidah Zaynab ؑ was two years younger. The children vowed to fast with their parents,

---

192 Sūrat al-Aʿrāf, verse 179.

193 Sūrat al-Qaṣaṣ, verse 77.

194 Sūrat al-Insān, verses 7-8.

and the three of them spent three days in hunger, shivering like little birds. Sayyidah Fāṭimah 🌸 had two bracelets. She gave them to Imām al-Ḥasan 🌸 and said, "Give them to my father Muḥammad and ask him to sell them and donate the money."

d. Instruction: Imām ʿAlī 🌸 told his son Imām al-Ḥasan 🌸, "The heart of a young child is like a plot of uncultivated land. It takes up whatever is put in it. This is why I began to instruct you before your heart became hard and your mind became preoccupied." When Imām al-Ḥasan's 🌸 mother died, he was between five and six years old, but people in the mosque treated him like a man. He used to hear the revelation from his grandfather 🌸 and repeat it back to his mother 🌸. A narration states that Imām ʿAlī 🌸 once hid in the house [to hear Imām al-Ḥasan 🌸 repeat the revelation]. Imām al-Ḥasan 🌸 wanted to repeat the revelation, but he became speechless. Sayyidah Fāṭimah 🌸 wondered at this so Imām al-Ḥasan 🌸 said, "O mother, my words are still few and my tongue did not aid me. Maybe a greater Master will keep me in His care."

e. Knowing Prophetic history: Imām al-Ṣādiq 🌸 focused greatly on this aspect when he said, "Teach your children of our knowledge something to benefit them" and "teach your children our *ḥadīths* before our opponents beat you to it." In our day, all sorts of movements beat the parents due to social media. This knowledge began with Abū Ṭālib, the faithful man of Quraysh. Imām al-Ṣādiq ﷷ said, "It pleased the Commander of the Believers to see the poetry of Abū Ṭālib recited and written down." Imām 'Alī ﷷ used to say, "Learn this poetry and teach it to your children. Abū Ṭālib was a follower of God's religion."

9 Muḥarram, 1443 A.H.

Two Sides of the Revolt of Justice Sayyidah al-Zahrāʾ and Imām al-Ḥusayn ﷺ

"Say, 'I do not ask you any reward for it except love of [my] relatives.'"[195]

Emotional Mobilization Resulting from Imām al-Ḥusayn's ﷺ Calamity

The phenomenon of mourning did not arise in the Buwayhid era like some researchers believe; it has been present since the time of the Prophet ﷺ. The author of *al-Ghadīr*, Shaykh al-Amīnī ﷺ, mentions in his book *Sīratunā wa-Sunnatunā*, that the Prophet ﷺ held eighteen mourning gatherings for Imām al-Ḥusayn ﷺ in the homes of Umm Salama, ʿĀʾisha, and Sayyidah Fāṭimah ﷺ. When Imām al-Ḥusayn ﷺ was born, the Prophet ﷺ became tearful, and when he ﷺ was asked about the reason, he ﷺ said that Jibrāʾīl told him ﷺ that his son Imām al-Ḥusayn ﷺ will be killed in Iraq by members of his ﷺ *umma*. Ibn Saʿd, Ibn Ḥajar al-Haytamī, Ibn Ḥajar al-ʿAsqalānī, Ibn ʿAsākir, Aḥmad b. Ḥanbal, and al-Ḥākim al-Tirmidhī mentioned three-hundred narrations stating that the Prophet Muḥammad held mourning gatherings for Imām al-Ḥusayn ﷺ ever since he ﷺ was born. The narrations that spoke of emotional mobilization for this issue are recurrent for the Shīʿa. One of the sound narrations is the one transmitted from Imām al-Riḍā ﷺ: "The day of

[195] Sūrat al-Shūrā, verse 23.

al-Ḥusayn made our eyelids sore, caused our tears to run, and humiliated our proud one in the land of Karb and Balā'. It left us with sorrow (*karb*) and tribulation (*balā'*) until the Last Day. Let the criers cry over one like al-Ḥusayn." Another narration is the following: "Abū 'Abdillāh [al-Ṣādiq] told me, 'O Abā 'Umāra, recite some poetry about al-Ḥusayn.' I did as he asked, and he cried. I recited more poetry and he cried again. By God, I kept reciting and he kept crying until I heard crying in the household. He then told me, 'O Abā 'Umāra, whoever recites poetry about al-Ḥusayn b. 'Alī and causes fifty people to cry earns Paradise, and whoever recites poetry about al-Ḥusayn b. 'Alī and causes thirty people to cry earns Paradise, and whoever recites poetry about al-Ḥusayn b. 'Alī and causes twenty people to cry earns Paradise, and whoever recites poetry about al-Ḥusayn b. 'Alī and causes ten people to cry earns Paradise, and whoever recites poetry about al-Ḥusayn b. 'Alī and causes one person to cry earns Paradise. Whoever recites poetry about al-Ḥusayn b. 'Alī and cries earns Paradise, and whoever recites poetry about al-Ḥusayn b. 'Alī and pretends to cry, earns Paradise."

There are two kinds of narrations that indicate great reward. Imām al-Riḍā ﷺ said, "Whoever remembers our calamity and cries for what was done to us will have the same degree as ours in Paradise on the Day of Judgment. Whoever reminds others of our calamity and cries and causes other people to cry will not cry on the day when all eyes will be tearful. Whoever sits in a gathering where we are being mentioned will not have his heart die on the day when all hearts die." Abū 'Abdillāh ﷺ said, "Whoever mentions us or hears us being mentioned and cries tears as few as a mosquito's wing will have his sins forgiven by God even if they were like the foam of the sea." The other kind of narrations highlight the spiritual value of crying over Imām al-Ḥusayn ﷺ. Abū 'Abdillāh ﷺ said, "The sigh of the person distressed over our oppression is glorification (*tasbīḥ*), his worry on our behalf is worship, and his keeping our secret is *jihād* in the way of God." All these narrations indicate the necessity of spiritual interaction with the cause of Imām al-Ḥusayn ﷺ; Imām al-Ṣādiq ﷺ even considered a sigh an act of glorification. All these are different kinds of interaction.

The Analytical View of Emotional Mobilization

Let us analyze such rewards. Is it plausible that a tear may be the cause for forgiving all sins and being with the Imāms ﷺ on the Day of Judgment? Some scholars attributed these narrations to the extremists (*al-ghulāt*), but this is not true. Scholarly logic requires us to have an analytical view. Some scholars stated that these narrations were false, so I will demonstrate the analytical view of the matter.

Many jurists focused on the dimension of worship and the fact that the Prophet ﷺ commanded us to hold fast to *al-thaqalayn*. We do not know the wisdom behind (all) acts of worship, but we still perform them. During the Abbasid era, the Shīʿa lived in fear and had no way to express their loyalty to Ahl al-Bayt 🕌 except through these rites. This is the historical dimension. The psychological dimension is based on the fact that every person needs to cry. A person needs to let pain out just as they need love because this decreases the pain of the spirit. Crying is a human need. These narrations, as well as certain verses, ensure the necessity of crying in having a sense of balance. The spiritual dimension is demonstrated by the fact that Imām Zayn al-ʿĀbidīn 🕌 cried for his father for thirty-four years. Whenever food and drink were laid out before him, he would say, "How can I drink when al-Ḥusayn was slaughtered?" In this, Imām Zayn al-ʿĀbidīn 🕌 was following his mother Sayyidah al-Zahrāʾ 🕌 who cried so much for the Prophet 🕌 that the people of Medina became bothered by it.

One of Imām Zayn al-ʿĀbidīn's 🕌 servants saw him crying while prostrating at night, so the Imām 🕌 told him that Yaʿqūb 🕌 had twelve sons, but when God 🕌 made one of them absent, Yaʿqūb 🕌 went blind with grief. The Imām 🕌 added that he saw his father, brother, and uncles all slaughtered. This is a reference to the verse: "They said, 'By God! You will go on remembering Yūsuf until you wreck your health or perish.'"[196] Crying is a complaint to God 🕌: "He said, 'I

---

[196] Sūrat Yūsuf, verse 85.

complain of my anguish and grief only to God. I know from God what you do not know.'"[197] If crying was also an act of worship, God ﷻ tells us, "Your Lord has said, 'Call Me, and I will hear you!'"[198] "When My servants ask you about Me, [tell them that] I am indeed nearmost. I answer the supplicant's call when he calls Me."[199] At the dimension of values, crying for Imām al-Ḥusayn ﵇ means interacting with Imām al-Ḥusayn ﵇ and remembering the values of sacrifice, dedication, and selflessness. Crying for Imām al-Ḥusayn ﵇ is a way of remembering these values.

The Philosophy of Ḥusaynī Rites

Why do these rites exist? Why do we relate them to Imām al-Ḥusayn ﵇ and his cause? The answer is at several levels.

1. The level of loyalty: "Say, 'I do not ask you any reward for it except *mawadda* of [my] relatives.'"[200] *Mawadda* is not just love but the demonstration of love. Participating in these gatherings is a demonstration of love.

---

[197] Sūrat Yūsuf, verse 86.

[198] Sūrat Ghāfir, verse 60.

[199] Sūrat al-Baqara, verse 186.

[200] Sūrat al-Shūrā, verse 23.

2. The religious level: Doesn't Imām al-Ḥusayn deserve that you stand by him every year? Why did Imām al-Ḥusayn revolt? "I did not revolt out of pride or arrogance." Imām al-Ḥusayn's movement was a movement of reform. From the religious perspective, all Muslims should stand with the movement of Imām al-Ḥusayn in application of the Qur'ān's call: "You are the best nation [ever] brought forth for mankind: you bid what is right and forbid what is wrong."[201] When the Prophet complained that no one was mourning over Ḥamza, all the people of Medina cried to honor him. Similarly, when Ja'far was killed, Sayyidah Fāṭimah cried for him.

3. The level of publicity: Any person who possesses a specific thought requires publicity that ingrains this thought in the minds of people. Sayyidah al-Zahrā' spoke of the pilgrimage as an establishment of religion, "Indeed Ṣafa and Marwa are among God's sacraments." *Sa'ī*, *ṭawāf*, and the throwing of the stones are acts of publicity that instill the principles of Islam in people's hearts. Muslims honor Islam greatly, and Ahl al-Bayt wanted the same thing for Karbalā'. All these rites are connected at the level of art, painting, and literature. Ahl al-Bayt wanted the voice of Imām al-Ḥusayn to remain heard.

---

[201] Sūrat āl-'Imrān, verse 110.

4. The political dimension: There was a political dimension behind these rites, which was unity. People of all skin colors, sects, and tribes become one under the call to prayer and the pilgrimage, and Ahl al-Bayt عليهم السلام wanted the same for Ashūrā'. In addition, these rites, whether they consisted of tears, chants, processions (*mawākib*, sing. *mawkib*), or marching to the grave of Imām al-Ḥusayn عليه السلام, are a protest against that horrible crime. Marching to the grave of Imām al-Ḥusayn عليه السلام is the biggest protest; al-Mutawakkil and others tried to put a stop to it, but it remained glorious forever.

10 Muḥarram, 1443 A.H.

The Crown of the Muslim Girl The Ḥijāb of Sayyidah Fāṭimah and Sayyidah Zaynab عليهما السلام

"And tell the faithful women to cast down their looks and to guard their private parts, and not to display their charms, except for what is outward."[202]

The Ḥijāb is a Qur'ānic Obligation

There is no difference between the *ḥijāb* and other religious responsibilities. Just like prayer is a Qur'ānic obligation, so is the *ḥijāb*. The Qur'ān used the same tone when mentioning the *ḥijāb* and obligation; I mean the imperative tone: "and let them draw their scarves over their bosoms;"[203] "O you who have faith! Prescribed for you is fasting as it was prescribed for those who were before you, so that you may be Godwary."[204] As for the parameters of the *ḥijāb*, we discussed them in three sessions this past Ramaḍān. The *ḥijāb* is a Qur'ānic obligation that has two characteristics. It is the right of God. The family may waive it, but the *ḥijāb* is not something like retribution (*qaṣāṣ*), which may be waived. The right of God may not be waived. The *ḥijāb* is a demonstration of servanthood to God and the connection to His religion and the law of the Qur'ān. In the same way, prayer and

---

202 Sūrat al-Nūr, verse 31.

203 Sūrat al-Nūr, verse 31.

204 Sūrat al-Baqara, verse 183.

fasting are a demonstration of servanthood to God regardless of whether the woman knows about the philosophy of the *ḥijāb* or not.

The Qur'ān mentioned the reasons and purposes of the *ḥijāb* just as it mentioned some other obligations: "And maintain the prayer. Indeed the prayer prevents indecencies and wrongs."[205] When the Qur'ān prohibited usury, it said, "O you who have faith! Be wary of God, and abandon [all claims to] what remains of usury, should you be faithful."[206] This means that the purpose of prohibiting usury is to prevent harm. "O wives of the Prophet! You are not like any other women: if you are wary [of God], then do not be complaisant in your speech, lest he in whose heart is a sickness should aspire;"[207] "O Prophet! Tell your wives and your daughters and the women of the faithful to draw closely over themselves their chadors [when going out]. That makes it likely for them to be recognized and not be troubled;"[208] "And let them not thump their feet to make known their hidden ornaments."[209]

---

205 Sūrat al-'Ankbūt, verse 45.

206 Sūrat al-Baqara, verse 278.

207 Sūrat al-Aḥzāb, verse 32.

208 Sūrat al-Aḥzāb, verse 59.

209 Sūrat al-Nūr, verse 31.

The Philosophy of the Ḥijāb

Based on these purposes, we begin this discussion. The philosophy of the *ḥijāb* is based on several pillars.

The social pillar: One of the theories of psychology is behaviorism. One of the points of behaviorism is responding to stimuli. These responses may be healthy or unhealthy, and the stimuli may be biological, sensory, or psychological. An example of responding to biological stimuli is eating when hungry. A healthy response remains within the limits of wellbeing; if the response becomes excessive, it is unhealthy. Sensory stimulants are displayed by the senses. An example is responding to sexual urges. If a person responds within certain limits, they are chaste, and if a person responds without limits, their response is unhealthy. An example of psychological stimuli is the following: every person is possessive. Possessing something within legal limits is healthy, while stealing is unhealthy. When the Qur'ān spoke of hypocrisy, it said, "There is a sickness in their hearts; then God increased their sickness."[210] This is a reference to an unhealthy response. The following is also an unhealthy response: "then do not be complaisant in your speech, lest he in whose heart is a sickness should aspire."[211]

---

[210] Sūrat al-Baqara, verse 10.

[211] Sūrat al-Aḥzāb, verse 32.

Having double standards is a widespread disease. There are women who wear the *ḥijāb* and engage in illegitimate relationships; these are double standards. Men who pant after women's make up and sweet voices have a disease too. These are widespread diseases in society. A woman who does not commit to the meaning of the *ḥijāb* should learn her social role from the Qur'ān: "Tell the faithful men to cast down their looks and to guard their private parts. That is more decent for them. God is indeed well aware of what they do. And tell the faithful women to cast down their looks and to guard their private parts, and not to display their charms."[212] Notice how God began with the men; men were given a function and then women. This is to guard society from the diseases that come from chasing desires.

The spiritual pillar: There is a school in psychology called introspection. Among its tenets is postponing pleasure. Pleasures are of several kinds: sensory, such as the pleasure of food, and psychological, such as the pleasure of love. The Prophet ﷺ said, "A believer loves and is loved." There are also mental pleasures. When a person solves complex problems and mathematical equations, they feel a certain pleasure. Postponement is also of several types; it can be related to compensation, value, and principle. The first type means postponing pleasure for a certain compensation. For example,

---

[212] Sūrat al-Nūr, verse 30-31.

during exams a student gives up food, sleep, and going out with friends. An example of postponement that is related to value is when a person does social volunteer work. It is a postponement of pleasure, but it is a valuable postponement because those who serve their communities are valued: "Among the faithful are men who fulfill what they have pledged to God;"[213] "men whom neither trading nor bargaining distracts from the remembrance of God, and the maintenance of prayer and the giving of *zakāt*."[214] Another kind of postponement is based on principle, and it is the most sophisticated kind of postponement. When you fast for fourteen hours, this is because you believe in a principle that gives you willpower and self-control: "O my son! Maintain the prayer and bid what is right and forbid what is wrong, and be patient through whatever may visit you. That is indeed the steadiest of courses."[215]

A woman instinctually loves to display her beauty and femininity, and she feels pleasure when someone praises her looks. Religion came and said, "Postpone this pleasure." The *ḥijāb* is a kind of postponement of pleasure that is based on principle. The *ḥijāb* is a display of willpower and impulse control. A girl who wears the *ḥijāb,* although her friends do not and although the

---

[213] Sūrat al-Aḥzāb, verse 23.

[214] Sūrat al-Nūr, verse 37.

[215] Sūrat Luqmān, verse 17.

media tells her to leave her *ḥijāb,* exercises postponement that reflects willpower: "As for him who was rebellious and preferred the life of this world, his refuge will indeed be hell. But as for him who is awed to stand before his Lord and forbids the soul from [following] desire, his refuge will indeed be paradise."[216]

The familial pillar: How do we preserve the familial atmosphere? Will Durant, in his book *Story of Civilization*, says that marriage is based on two inclinations. A man's inclination is to possess the woman, while the woman naturally likes to act coy around the man. This preserves the marital home. An intimate loving relationship, based on these two pillars, guarantees the longevity of the home. However, if women freely offered themselves up and the men were able to see their charms anywhere, the relationship between the two sides directly changes from emotional to sexual. In this case, the emotional bond between a man and his wife becomes weak, and the family goes into a standstill because the man is encountering many types of temptations. How then can we preserve the marital home? This happens when a man's pleasure is limited to his wife, whether in looks, touches, and romantic dates. If a man's pleasures are limited to the wife, the relationship becomes an intimate, personal relationship. Let's look at the West. The men found alternatives to their wives, and the emotional flame

---

[216] Sūrat ʿAbasa, verses 37-40.

between couples was extinguished. For this reason, if a woman safeguards her *ḥijāb*, she is doing a favor to society as a whole.

Someone might ask, "Why are you making a big deal out of this? Men get used to seeing temptations with time. Are men so full of lust? The more a man is used to seeing women everywhere in all their variations, he will get used to it and his sex drive will decrease." The philosopher Russel says that there are two kinds of needs: temporary needs like the need to sleep that is fulfilled after seven or eight hours or the need for food that is fulfilled when a person is full. The other needs are permanent needs, such as the love of money. Imām ʿAlī ☙ says, "There are two gluttons that are never satisfied: the seeker of knowledge and the seeker of money." Sexual addiction is a renewable need; every time it is aroused, it surges again. Sexual addiction is not the same as regular sexual intercourse, where the person has sex and then becomes calm again. Sexual addiction never goes away and the man never "gets used to it."

Sāmī ʿĀmirī conducted a study that was published in the *New York Times* on the magical powers of visual perception. The author conducted multiple interviews, and found that companies and manufacturers spend millions of dollars to have women displayed on their products; women in lingerie or bathing suits, or women showing their legs or their breasts. All of this is done to put women on display. Women are even used in advertisements for regular kinds of beverages because they have a magical effect on men. Would women spend one dollar to have men displayed like this? The millions that are spent highlight the extent of women's charms on men. Undoubtedly, this weakens the familial relationship.

The mystical basis: Might (*'izza*) is an attribute of God: "Yet all might belongs to God."[217] It means the combination of His beauty and majesty. God's mercy, forgiveness, and providence (*rizq*) belong to the attributes of beauty, and power and knowledge belong to the attributes of majesty. Human beings too can combine beauty and majesty. Women are a clear example of this. Women, by nature, are works of beauty, so to reach might, they should combine beauty with majesty. The way to achieve this is by dressing modestly. Covering beauty up is power, transcendence, and elevation. This makes the woman mighty. Vulgar women are cheap, while chaste women preserve their transcendence by covering up their beauty.

"I'm Free: I Was Never Forced"

Such women say, "I'm free to display my beauty. It's a right of mine to choose whether to wear the *ḥijāb* or not." Do human values include absolute freedom? A woman's freedom is worthy if it is coupled with dignity.

[217] Sūrat al-Munāfiqūn, verse 8.

One of the best values, for instance, is knowledge. If a society wanted to remain ignorant, would freedom be a value here? An example is the Coronavirus . If society decided that it did not want to take any precautions, is freedom a worthy value here? "Certainly We have honored the Children of Adam, and carried them over land and sea, and provided them with all the good things, and given them an advantage over many of those We have created with a complete preference."[218] A woman is a source of giving and light.

Modest Without the Veil?

"There are women who are chaste without wearing the *ḥijāb*. Aren't chastity and modesty important too? Why do you focus on appearances? Why don't you focus on the inside?" It is because might is a combination of the outside and the inside. An example is prayer: "Maintain the prayer. Indeed the prayer prevents indecencies and wrongs."[219] If I don't commit indecencies and wrongs, why should I pray? The moral value appears through prayer; the value of worship combines internal and external dimensions. Another example is fornication: "Do not approach fornication. It is indeed an indecency and an evil way."[220] You [religious people] say that

[218] Sūrat al-Isrā', verse 70.

[219] Sūrat al-'Ankbūt, verse 45.

[220] Sūrat al-Isrā', verse 32.

fornication leads to a mixing up of lineages, but what if a woman uses birth control pills or what if a man is infertile? Is it fornication then? Chastity is refraining from such illegitimate relationships: "O wives of the Prophet! You are not like any other women: if you are wary [of God], then do not be complaisant in your speech, lest he in whose heart is a sickness should aspire, and speak honorable words. Stay in your houses and do not display your finery with the display of the former [days of] ignorance. Maintain the prayer and pay the *zakāt*, and obey God and His Apostle."[221] Although piety is piety of the heart, the verse obligated women to display it through behavior, giving precedence to the *ḥijāb* over prayer.

The media as a pillar: in sociology and administration, the media is an important element, and symbols are of its important components. Symbols are more powerful than explicitness. Islam too paid attention to symbols. Symbols may be structures, jobs, or specific clothes. A dome, for example, is a symbol of a place of worship, a minaret is a symbol of Islamic identity, the symbol of doctors is a white coat, soldiers wear military uniforms, and pilgrims wear *iḥrām* clothes to symbolize putting the world and its excesses aside. In prayer, women wear the *ḥijāb* even if they were praying alone or in the presence of a *maḥram* as a display of courtesy, and throwing the stones during the pilgrimage is a symbol of

[221] Sūrat al-Aḥzāb, verses 32-33.

casting Satan away. In the West, a woman who wears the *ḥijāb* displays her Islamic religious identity and her pride in this identity.

Parents have a religious duty of monitoring their daughters and sons. Monitor your sons' behavior, and monitor your daughters' commitment to the *ḥijāb*. The family must care about such things: "O you who have faith! Save yourselves and your families from a Fire."[222] This requires publicity and not just jurisprudence. We must publicize the culture of *ḥijāb* through drawings, billboards, movies, and series. We need to make the culture of *ḥijāb* mainstream by displaying the *ḥijāb's* philosophy and purposes.

The Educational Values of Karbalā'

Karbalā' is not simply a bloody battle involving combat and the martyrdom of a group of people for the sake of their values. Karbalā' is a school of human ideals and values that teaches commitment to the *ḥijāb*. Sayyidah Zaynab ﷺ stood before Yazīd b. Muʿāwiya and rebuked him for violating the *ḥijāb*: "Is it fair, you son of freed-captives, that you cover up your women, both free and slaves, while you take the daughters of the Prophet of God as captives? You violated their covers and put their faces on display, making their enemies drive them from place to place while travelers and people at waterholes

[222] Sūrat al-Taḥrīm, verse 6.

look at them, and those near and far, absent and present, and lowly and noble stare at their faces."

Karbalāʾ also teaches selflessness. Al-ʿAbbās عليه السلام had access to water, but he عليه السلام remembered the thirst of his brother [Imām al-Ḥusayn عليه السلام] and threw the water away: "By God, this is not the act of my religion, nor the act of someone who is true in his certainty." Another lesson is committing to principles: "I am ʿAlī b. al-Ḥusayn b. ʿAlī. By the House of God, we are worthier of the Prophet;" "I am al-Ḥusayn b. ʿAlī. I swore that I will not bend;" "Indeed, the bastard son of the bastard has settled on two things: either war or humiliation, and humiliation is far from us." Karbalāʾ also teaches cooperation between the young man, the small boy, the woman, and the old man. Ḥabīb was an old man, ʿAlī al-Akbar was a young man, al-Qāsim was a boy, and Sukayna was a woman. Another lesson is absolute connection to God. Imām al-Ḥusayn's عليه السلام son was slaughtered while he عليه السلام held him, so he عليه السلام lifted him to the sky and said, "What befell me is easier to bear because God sees it." When the arrow struck Imām al-Ḥusayn's عليه السلام heart, he did not groan with pain. Instead, he عليه السلام said, "O God, I am content with Your decree." When Sayyidah Zaynab عليها السلام reached Imām al-Ḥusayn's عليه السلام dismembered body, she held the body up while her brother's عليه السلام remains fell from her hands and she said, "O God, accept this offering from us."

11 Muḥarram, 1443 A.H.

Heiress of Sayyidah al-Zahrā' عليها السلام al-'Aqīla Zaynab عليها السلام

"Indeed We have given you abundance. So pray to your Lord, and sacrifice [the sacrificial camel]. Indeed it is your enemy who is without posterity."[223]

Sūrat al-Kawthar is one of the blessings God gave to the Prophet ﷺ. There are many other verses that mentioned these blessings: "Did He not find you an orphan, and shelter you? Did He not find you astray, and guide you? Did He not find you needy, and enrich you?"[224] "Did We not open your chest and relieve you of your burden?"[225] There are three explanations for the word *al-kawthar*. The first is that it means great abundance, and that God ﷻ gave the Prophet ﷺ unique stations in this world and the next. The second explanation is that it is an *Arabized* word of the Hebrew *al-kushar*, which means purity and integrity. The third explanation is that *al-kawthar* is none other than Sayyidah Fāṭimah al-Zahrā' عليها السلام. This is the explanation of our Imāms عليهم السلام. In fact, Sayyidah Fāṭimah al-Zahrā' عليها السلام encompasses all three explanations because they all apply to her. Eleven Imāms عليهم السلام descended from her, and this is great abundance. She عليها السلام is also a manifestation of purity; who is purer than her? She is one of the five referred to in the verse: "Indeed God desires to repel all impurity from you, O People of the Household, and purify you

---

[223] Sūrat al-Kawthar, verses 1-3.

[224] Sūrat al-Ḍuḥā, verses 6-8.

[225] Sūrat al-Sharḥ, verses 1-2.

with a thorough purification."[226] Her children are in great abundance, and one of her children is al-ʿAqīla Zaynab ﷺ.

The Life of al-ʿAqīla Zaynab ﷺ

al-ʿAqīla Zaynab ﷺ was born either on 5 Jumādā al-Ūlā during year five of the Hijra or on 6 Shaʿbān during year 6 of the Hijra. She ﷺ died a few months after her brother Imām al-Ḥusayn ﷺ because his ﷺ death took a toll on her ﷺ. She ﷺ was fifty-five when she ﷺ died; she ﷺ is two years younger than Imām al-Ḥusayn ﷺ. Sayyidah Zaynab ﷺ was buried either in Shām or in Egypt, and for the Imāms the more probable place is Shām. She ﷺ had two privileges: the first is descending from the proud loins and the pure wombs like Imām al-Ḥusayn ﷺ: "The Jāhiliyya did not make you impure with its impurities and it did not clothe you with any of its darknesses." The second privilege is the privilege of education; she lived with five of the infallibles and inherited their knowledge. Ibn ʿAbbās narrated from her although he was a scholar in his own right: "Our ʿAqīla Zaynab told me that the Commander of the Believers..." She ﷺ also narrated her mother's ﷺ lengthy sermon.

One narration states that Imām ʿAlī ﷺ did not name her ﷺ himself but waited for the Prophet ﷺ to name her

---

226 Sūrat al-Aḥzāb, verse 33.

ﷺ. The Prophet ﷺ was awaiting the command from heaven to name her, and Jibrā'īl told him ﷺ to call her Zaynab ﷺ. The word *zaynab* either means a kind of tree that smells nice and is pleasant to look at, or a father's adornment (*zaynu ab*), which then became one word (*zaynab*). The Prophet Muḥammad ﷺ cried when Jibrā'īl told him ﷺ that her ﷺ life will be filled with sorrow. A narration states that when Imām ʿAlī ﷺ told her about her future, she smiled and said, "My mother already told me." She was raised up in knowledge, eloquence, courage, and patience.

The governor of Medina wrote to Yazīd something along the lines of: "If you want Medina to yourself, be careful. Sayyidah Zaynab bt. ʿAlī is a wise and intelligent woman, and she and her people have set their minds on avenging al-Ḥusayn." Sayyidah Zaynab ﷺ married ʿAbdullāh b. Jaʿfar al-Ṭayyār and had several children with him; they were four boys and a girl: ʿAbbās, ʿAwn, ʿAlī, Muḥammad, and Umm Kulthūm.

Her Heroism

In psychology there is a branch that is concerned with the character. Characters are of three types: the classic character that lives a life of routine without development or creativity, the special character that is different and distinguished either at the level of minds, careers, eloquence, or art such that each character shines in its own way. The last is the unique character that possesses several traits allowing it to shine in several domains. Can a person shine in medicine and in art as well? Both domains require time, practical effort, and energy. If a person can combine several domains, we say that they are unique.

Imām ʿAlī combined opposites in his character: he shone in his worship and shone in battle. Excelling in worship requires time and effort; Imām ʿAlī used to pray a thousand *rakʿas* every day and night. Excelling in battle also requires time. Imām ʿAlī combined opposites in his character; he was the leader of a state, monitoring its course and apparatuses while praying a thousand *rakʿas*. He also gave sermons and spread knowledge and education while being the leader in battle. How was he able to combine these traits? His beloved daughter Sayyidah Zaynab was also like him in this regard; she was like several people in one. She was eloquent, as though speaking with her father's tongue. She was also brave, without worry or fear, and she possessed an administrative ability that became clear after Ashūrāʾ. Let's speak of the distinct characters that Sayyidah Zaynab possessed.

The first is the knowledgeable character. The infallible Imām [Zayn al-ʿĀbidīn] said to her, "O aunt, you are knowledgeable without being taught and you understand without someone making you understand."

Knowledge has two types: acquired knowledge (*ʿilm iktisābī*) that comes in detail from a specific source, and bestowed knowledge (*ʿilm ladunī*) that involves knowing the details of things through inspiration: "and He has taught you what you did not know;"[227] "and taught him a knowledge from Our own."[228] This means that bestowed knowledge is an encyclopedia of knowledge. Certain texts introduce us to this character. On the eleventh day of Muḥarram, Imām al-Sajjād became anxious when he looked at the bloodied bodies of his relatives. Sayyidah Zaynab asked him, "Why do I see you on the verge of death, O remainder of my grandfather, father, and brothers?" Imām al-Sajjād said, "How could I not panic and become anxious when I saw the bodies of my master, brothers, uncles, cousins, and family members covered in their own blood, out in the open air? Their garments were stolen, and no one shrouded them or buried them in the earth. No one stopped to look at them, and no human being came anywhere near them, as though they were some people from Daylam and al-Khazar."

Sayyidah Zaynab said to Imām al-Sajjād, "Do not panic at what you are seeing. By God, it was foretold by the Prophet of God to your grandfather, father, and uncle. God took the pledge of some people of this

---

[227] Sūrat al-Nisā', verse 113.

[228] Sūrat al-Kahf, verse 65.

umma although its Pharaohs don't recognize them. They are known by the inhabitants of the heavens who will gather up these dispersed and bloody bodies and bury them, erecting in al-Ṭaff a landmark for the grave of your father, the master of martyrs. This grave will never disappear as nights and days follow one another. By God, the Imāms of unbelief and the supporters of misguidance will indeed strive to erase and eliminate this landmark, but it will only become more visible and elevated." This is an example of Sayyidah Zaynab's bestowed knowledge.

The other example is when ʿUbayd Allāh b. Ziyād addressed Sayyidah Zaynab. She had put on her shabbiest clothes so that she wouldn't be recognized, but the women and children kept flocking around her. ʿUbayd Allāh b. Ziyād asked, "Who is that woman?" He was told that she was Sayyidah Zaynab, so he asked, "What did you think of what God did to your brother?" Ibn Ziyād was an advocate of fatalism (*al-jabr*), so he was saying that everything that had occurred in Karbalāʾ happened due to God's unchangeable will: God wanted us to become rulers. The Umayyads were saying, "God gave us victory over you. If you were right, He would have given you victory instead. If your brother was right, why was he killed? What did you think of what God did to him?" Sayyidah Zaynab said, "I saw nothing but beauty." She meant that Ibn Ziyād was only imagining that this was a defeat. In fact, it was a victory of principles.

The second is the mystical character. Sayyidah Zaynab 𝖺 is made of pure worship; how could she not be when her father is the Commander of the Believers 𝖺 and her mother 𝖺 is the woman of the prayer niche? It is said that Sayyidah Zaynab 𝖺 reached a degree of peace. There is a view rooted in sovereignty and a view rooted in dominion. Anyone who views existence through the view of dominion reaches the station of peace: "Thus did We show Abraham the dominions of the heavens and the earth, that he might be of those who possess certitude;"[229] "So immaculate is He in whose hand is the dominion of all things and to whom you shall be brought back."[230]

Sayyidah Zaynab 𝖺 became a manifestation of the verse: "'O soul at peace! Return to your Lord, pleased, pleasing!"[231] This reflected in her sayings and actions. When Imām al-Ḥusayn 𝖺 was killed, this woman came out of the tents dragging her garments behind her and walked to Imām al-Ḥusayn's 𝖺 body. Although she 𝖺 lost two sons of her own, she 𝖺 did not cry. She 𝖺 put her hands under the body and said, "O God, accept this offering from us." Seeing beauty requires a beautiful spirit. Diseased spirits, on the other hand, do not see beauty: "Be beautiful and you will find existence

---

229 Sūrat al-Anʿām, verse 75.

230 Sūrat Yā Sīn, verse 83.

231 Sūrat al-Fajr, verse 27-28.

beautiful." Spite, hatred, worry, and fear stop a person from seeing beauty: "So be patient, with a patience that is beautiful."[232]

The third is the active character. This character differs from the passive character by having a project. People who possess this character watch, keep up with events, and plan all at once. Sayyidah Zaynab is a person who had projects. When 'Abdullāh b. 'Abbās asked Imām al-Ḥusayn, "Why are you going out to Iraq when they betrayed your father and brother?" Sayyidah Zaynab turned to him and asked, "How can you advise our master to go out and leave us behind?" Who can withstand the events of the tenth day of Muḥarram? History has never mentioned a woman who did all this: calming the children, receiving the bodies, gathering the orphans, nursing the sick, saying farewell to the heroes [before they went out to battle], and giving Imām al-Ḥusayn spiritual support. Sayyidah Zaynab's role was not limited to Karbalā'.

Imām al-Ḥusayn had two successors: an apparent successor and an actual successor. The actual successor was Imām Zayn al-'Ābidīn and the apparent successor was Sayyidah Zaynab. People went back to Sayyidah Zaynab in their affairs; Imām al-Ḥusayn gave her this position for several reasons. One reason is so that she may guard Imām Zayn al-'Ābidīn.

---

[232] Sūrat al-Ma'ārij, verse 5 (translation changed slightly).

Another reason is her social position. Sayyidah Zaynab was more socially important than Imām Zayn al-'Ābidīn because she was the daughter of 'Alī and Sayyidah Fāṭimah. She put the gloaters and enemies in their place, and she stopped people who came to give Ahl al-Bayt charity, saying, "It is prohibited for us to receive charity." She experienced the hardship of captivity. The caravan driver was going quickly to reach Kūfa as soon as possible, and a narration states that the skins peeled off of Ahl al-Bayt's faces due to the burning heat of the sun. Sayyidah Zaynab withstood all of this; she neither collapsed or weakened. Sayyidah Zaynab was brought into Yazīd's presence with a rope tied around her neck to make her appear weak and humiliated, but she never weakened: "I think too little of you to do something as great as rebuke you; I am not under the illusion that words will affect you."

The fourth is the character capable of publicity. In her book *Zaynab Baṭalat Karbalā'*, 'Ā'isha Bint al-Shāṭi' says that without Sayyidah Zaynab, al-Ḥusayn's movement would have disappeared. Every movement requires publicity. Sayyidah Zaynab's words were her means of publicity. The Umayyads wanted to extinguish this revolution and they put Ahl al-Bayt under close surveillance. However, Sayyidah Zaynab made use of her captivity, and put her voice in service of al-Ḥusayn's revolution until she exposed the crime of the Umayyads, particularly in Kūfa. This resulted in the movement of the penitents (*al-tawwābūn*), the movement of al-Mukhtār, the movement of Zayd b. 'Alī, and the movement of Muḥammad b. al-Ḥasan. All these movements were an extension of Sayyidah Zaynab's ﷺ voice. She is a unique person who was a representation of her father the Commander of the Believers ﷺ. Literary authors know that if you compare the sermons of Sayyidah al-Zahrā' ﷺ, the Commander of the Believers ﷺ, and Sayyidah Zaynab ﷺ, you will notice the same literary style. They ﷺ used the same terms, which would make you believe the speaker was one. Prophet Muḥammad's ﷺ style of speech was different; Imām al-Ḥusayn's ﷺ style of speech was different.

The Elevated Meanings in Sayyidah Zaynab's ﷺ Sermon

When Sayyidah Zaynab ﷺ entered into Yazīd's presence, she saw that his court included Jews, Christians, rulers of other states, and people of all sorts because Yazīd was the head of the state. Sayyidah Zaynab ﷺ made use of the circumstances and said, "Did you think, O Yazīd, when you controlled the ends of the earth and the horizons of the sky, and paraded us around like prisoners, that God preferred you over us? Did you think this happened because God holds you in high regard, so you turned up your nose and admired yourself? You were overjoyed when you saw the world going your way and matters happening as you pleased, taking what belongs to us and our usurping authority. But wait! Did you forget God's saying, 'Let the faithless not suppose that the respite that We grant them is good for their souls: We give them respite only that they may increase in sin, and there is a humiliating punishment for them'?"[233]

"Hāshim toyed with the kingship, and no revelation came down." This is what Yazīd said. As for Sayyidah Zaynab ﷺ, she told him, "Is it fair, you son of freed-captives, that you cover up your women, both free and slaves, while you take the daughters of the Prophet of God as captives? You violated their covers and put their faces on display, making their enemies drive them from place to place while travelers and people at waterholes look at them, and those near and far, absent and present, and lowly and noble stare at their faces. There is no guardian of their men among them, or a protector of their kin. You did all this in defiance to God and ingratitude to the Prophet and refusal of what he brought from God. One does not wonder at you or feel astonished at what you did. And yet, how might we hope for discretion from those whose mouths spit out the livers of the martyrs and whose flesh grew on the blood of the blessed?"

---

233 Sūrat āl-'Imrān, verse 178.

In Kūfa, Sayyidah Zaynab ﷺ stirred up the people's feelings and stood before them. These people knew Sayyidah Zaynab ﷺ, so when they saw her ﷺ, they began to cry. She ﷺ said to them, "You people of treachery, betrayal, and disappointment. May your tears never stop and may your moans never cease. You are like her who would undo her yarn, breaking it up after [spinning it to] strength by making your oaths a means of [mutual] deceit among yourselves. Is there anything among you except excessiveness, arrogance, and terrible hatred?" She ﷺ was pointing out their faults. She ﷺ continued, "Woe to you. Do you know which beloved of Muḥammad you have butchered, which pledge you have broken, which honored daughter of Muḥammad you have stripped of covering, which sanctity of his you have violated, and which blood of his you have spilled? ... Do you wonder at the sky raining blood? 'Yet the punishment of the Hereafter is surely more disgraceful, and they will not be helped.'[234] Do not be overjoyed at the break you've been given, for God is not obliged to act swiftly."

12 Muḥarram, 1443 A.H.

---

[234] Sūrat Fuṣṣilat, verse 16.

www.ingramcontent.com/pod-product-compliance
Lightning Source LLC
Chambersburg PA
CBHW031511120626
46545CB00005B/1829